WE[LCOME]

Have you eve[r wondered why your cat] follows you [around but on other days they're] completely disinterested? Why they sit on your laptop when you're trying to work or drink from the tap instead of their water bowl?

While some people think cats are aloof and unaffectionate, others find them playful and cuddly. All cats are different, but if you really want to know what they're thinking and why they behave the way they do then all you have to do is pay attention.

This book is your ultimate guide to understanding your moggy. Learn how to speak cat chat, understand their body language and decode their strange or bad behaviour. From training them to finding out how to keep them happy throughout their lives, you'll not only get to know your kitty better, but you'll also discover the benefits of owning one of these fascinating felines.

FUTURE

WHAT YOUR CAT IS TRYING TO TELL YOU

Future PLC Quay House, The Ambury, Bath, BA1 1UA

Editorial
Editor **Zara Gaspar**
Art Editor **Madelene King**
Compiled by **Alice Pattillo & Laurie Newman**
Senior Art Editor **Andy Downes**
Head of Art & Design **Greg Whitaker**
Editorial Director **Jon White**
Managing Director **Grainne McKenna**

Contributors
Becky Bradbury, Ella Carter, Jo Cole, Natalie Denton, Bee Ginger, Philippa Grafton, Laura Jaques, Adam Millward, Jo Stass, Vicky Williams

Cover images
Getty Images

Photography
All copyrights and trademarks are recognised and respected

Advertising
Media packs are available on request
Commercial Director **Clare Dove**

International
Head of Print Licensing **Rachel Shaw**
licensing@futurenet.com
www.futurecontenthub.com

Circulation
Head of Newstrade **Tim Mathers**

Production
Head of Production **Mark Constance**
Production Project Manager **Matthew Eglinton**
Advertising Production Manager **Joanne Crosby**
Digital Editions Controller **Jason Hudson**
Production Managers **Keely Miller, Nola Cokely, Vivienne Calvert, Fran Twentyman**

Printed in the UK

Distributed by Marketforce, 5 Churchill Place, Canary Wharf, London, E14 5HU
www.marketforce.co.uk – For enquiries, please email: mfcommunications@futurenet.com

What Your Cat is Trying to Tell You Second Edition (LBZ5536)
© 2023 Future Publishing Limited

We are committed to only using magazine paper which is derived from responsibly managed, certified forestry and chlorine-free manufacture. The paper in this bookazine was sourced and produced from sustainable managed forests, conforming to strict environmental and socioeconomic standards.

All contents © 2023 Future Publishing Limited or published under licence. All rights reserved. No part of this magazine may be used, stored, transmitted or reproduced in any way without the prior written permission of the publisher. Future Publishing Limited (company number 2008885) is registered in England and Wales. Registered office: Quay House, The Ambury, Bath BA1 1UA. All information contained in this publication is for information only and is, as far as we are aware, correct at the time of going to press. Future cannot accept any responsibility for errors or inaccuracies in such information. You are advised to contact manufacturers and retailers directly with regard to the price of products/services referred to in this publication. Apps and websites mentioned in this publication are not under our control. We are not responsible for their contents or any other changes or updates to them. This magazine is fully independent and

Future plc is a public company quoted on the London Stock Exchange (symbol: FUTR)
www.futureplc.com

Chief Executive **Jon Steinberg**
Non-Executive Chairman **Richard Huntingford**
Chief Financial and Strategy Officer **Penny Ladkin-Brand**

Tel +44 (0)1225 442 244

CONTENTS

8
ABOUT CATS
Fierce predator to favourite pet – cats in a nutshell

14
OWNER'S GUIDE
Everything you need to know when getting a new cat

18
CATS AND THEIR HUMANS
Uncover the relationship between you and your pet

21
6 WAYS YOU CAN TELL YOUR CAT LOVES YOU
Discover how cats communicate their affection

22
HOW SMART ARE CATS?
Is it time to reassess what we think we know about our moggy's mind?

28
CAT CHAT
Decoding the hidden messages in the sounds your kitty makes

30
CAT BODY LANGUAGE
The best way to understand your cat is to watch them

38
WHY DOES MY CAT DO THAT?
The mystery meanings behind your feline's strange behaviours

46
HOW TO STROKE YOUR CAT
Petting can be a wonderful way of building a strong bond between you and your cat

48
ACROCATS
Discover the secret to your cat's incredible agility

54
MISBEHAVIOUR EXPLAINER
Could your cat's bad behaviour be a sign that something is troubling them?

60
CAT MYTHS
Some of the most common cat myths debunked

66
HOW TO TRAIN YOUR CAT
They may not be as easy to teach as dogs but there are many tricks they can master

68
CATS AND CHILDREN
Make sure your kids and kitty form a close bond and grow up the best of friends

72
DOES YOUR CAT HAVE FEELINGS?
Which of our emotions do cats share and how do they express these?

77
5 REASONS YOUR CAT FOLLOWS YOU AROUND
Find out why your cat is seemingly always only a few footsteps behind you

78
BECOME A CAT WHISPERER
Learn how to have better chat with your cat

86
HOW CATS SEE HUMANS
Does your cat recognise your face and how do they really feel about you?

90
SIGNS YOUR CAT MAY BE ILL
Keep an eye out for these warning signs

92
HOW TO KEEP YOUR CAT HAPPY
The best way to ensure you have a carefree cat

98
YOUR CAT'S FAVOURITE THINGS
From tasty treats to toasty naps, discover what it is your cat can't resist

100
5 THINGS TO NEVER DO
Be your cat's protector and never do any of these things

102
BREED BEHAVIOUR
Take a prowl into the world of feline characteristics

113
5 THINGS YOUR CAT WANTS YOU TO KNOW
What your kitty is trying to communicate

114
YOUR CAT'S PET HATES
Discover the things that get on your cat's whiskers

120
YOUR CAT'S SIXTH SENSE
From earthquakes to cancer, our cats often know what's going on before we do

126
BENEFITS OF HAVING A CAT
How having a cat can be good for you and your health

ALL ABOUT DOMESTIC CATS

Never quite forgetting their wild origins, domestic cats manage to strut a fine line between fierce predator and loving pet

WORDS VICTORIA WILLIAMS

THE HISTORY OF A PURR-FECT PARTNERSHIP

While they can often behave as though they deem humans to be inferior, cats actually make for brilliant companions, and they've been by our side for millennia

With their independence, frequent aloofness and tendency to wander off for hours – or even days – at a time, cats don't sound like ideal pets, and yet they're one of the most popular animals on the planet. Thanks to the adoration of self-confessed 'cat people', they've claimed many hearts, homes and YouTube views.

Their attitude towards humans is unlike that of any other pet, and that's partly because their history with us is a little different to the domestication story of other species. While people captured and kept animals such as pigs, birds and dogs, cats have always sauntered in and out of our lives. When humans started farming and storing grains over 10,000 years ago, rodents were naturally attracted to the huge quantities of food. This, in turn, naturally drew African wild cats to settlements. The relationship worked for both parties; the cats had plentiful access to prey and the farmers' crops were protected from vermin.

Once the cats became tame enough for people to get close to them, they were taken to other continents until they were all over the globe. Their role gradually developed from pest controllers to companions, and different breeds with distinct characteristics began to emerge, but they've all retained a streak of wildness.

Kittens are born with a set of predatory instincts that they develop as they play with their mother and siblings. These instincts are so ingrained in a cat's brain that they govern the actions of even the most laid-back of moggies. Lots of their amusing and baffling behaviour makes a lot more sense when you consider the lifestyles of their wild cousins: climbing to high spots gives them a good vantage point for surveying the area, and scratching your sofa spreads their scent and keeps their claws in good shape. Even their peculiar love of cardboard boxes can be explained, as confined spaces provide security and strategic hiding places for avoiding predators and ambushing prey.

Cats aren't aloof – they form close and loving bonds with their owners

COAT COLOURATION
Cats come in all sorts of colours and patterns, from pure white to striped tabbies and the leopard-like rosettes of the Bengal cat. The combined effects of multiple genes control the texture, pattern and colours of each cat's coat.

"KITTENS ARE BORN WITH A SET OF PREDATORY INSTINCTS THAT THEY DEVELOP AS THEY PLAY WITH THEIR MOTHER AND SIBLINGS"

INSIDE THE CAT

Even after thousands of years of domestication and selective breeding, domestic cats still share many features with their wild relatives that make them efficient predators and expert acrobats

PINPOINT HEARING
Cats have an acute sense of hearing and can detect sounds at higher frequencies than dogs can hear.

PRECISION EAR CONTROL
Cats' ears contain 32 muscles each and can be rotated 180 degrees and moved independently.

SEEING IN THE DARK
Cats have a wider field of view and much better nighttime vision than us, but they cannot see as many colours as us..

NO NOSE IS ALIKE
Just like humans, every cat has a unique print – theirs is in the pattern of bumps on their noses.

TEETH FOR TEARING
Adult cats have 30 teeth. As they've evolved to eat almost nothing but meat, they lack specialised grinding teeth.

FEELING THEIR WAY
Sensitive whiskers enable cats to gather information about their environment and judge whether they'll fit in a space.

SMELLING WITH THEIR MOUTH
On the roof of a cat's mouth is the Jacobson's organ, an extra scent organ that detects chemical signals.

CLAWS OUT

A cat's claws are attached to the last bone on each toe. Usually they're sheathed within the toe pad, but the cat can contract ligaments in the feet to quickly extend them. Claws are useful for hunting, climbing and fighting, but they'd get tangled and worn down if they were permanently exposed.

Retracted *Extended*

> INFANCY

Tiny and helpless *0 days*
Kittens are born blind, deaf and unable to stand. They huddle together and feed frequently on mum's milk.

On their feet *3 weeks*
By now a kitten will begin to walk, keeping their tail upright to balance them. Their canine teeth now begin to emerge.

Honing their skills *5 weeks*
By five weeks old, kittens have a fully developed set of senses and can run, climb, play, jump and try to clean themselves.

> JUVENILE

Moving home *8 weeks*
At this age kittens are taken to new homes, but a few extra weeks allows them to develop socially with their family.

Little hunters *4 months*
After four months, permanent adult teeth begin to replace baby teeth. Their hunting instinct is now fully developed.

MULTIPURPOSE TAIL
Almost ten per cent of a cat's bones are in its tail, which provides balance and communicates the cat's mood.

DIGESTIVE SYSTEM
The digestive system is short, reducing the weight a cat carries in order to keep it light and agile.

LAYERS OF FUR
A cat's coat is made up of long, stiff guard hairs, short, soft down hairs and awn hairs, which are what contain most of the colouration.

While most cats are covered in thick fur, Sphynx cats have such fine hairs that they appear hairless. Without fur to keep them warm or protect them, Sphynx cats like to be near heat sources but can't spend too much time in the sun.

PROTECTIVE EXTRA SKIN
Loose skin lets cats squirm away from danger, and a thick flap of belly skin called the primordial pouch protects them during fights, reducing the risk of injury.

SWEATING THROUGH THEIR FEET
The only places on a cat's body that produce sweat are the pads on the bottom of their feet.

ALWAYS ON THEIR TOES
Cats walk on their toes and use a rare pacing gait shared with giraffes and camels.

DID YOU KNOW?
A male cat is called a tom. A female cat is called a molly, while a pregnant or nursing female is known as a queen.

MATURITY

All grown up *4–12 months*
Unneutered female cats reach sexual maturity at around four months, and males are able to breed from seven months.

Having kittens *4 months+*
Pregnancy lasts for nine to ten weeks. Litters usually consist of three to five kittens, but litters of as many as 15 do occur.

Getting serious *1 year+*
Adult cats play less than kittens, spending more of their time sleeping, cleaning and exploring. The many different personalities of cats are most evident in adults.

Slowing down *8 years+*
After eight years cats are considered 'senior'. Like humans they begin to experience health problems, and they will spend even more time sleeping.

INSIDE AND OUT

Cats are adored the world over and make an effort to return the love, but they're just a step away from returning to their wild state

Cats have been admired – sometimes revered – for thousands of years by many human cultures. They might not always show us the same level of respect, but when the mood takes them, many make it clear that they enjoy being around people. Even their alarming habit of bringing dead animals into the home is meant with affection; in the wild, cats bring injured or dead prey to their young in order to teach them to hunt, so the mangled mouse left on the floor is just your pet's way of trying to help you survive. Bless.

They're capable of making many different sounds, but the cat's best-known vocalisation is meowing. It may come as a surprise to learn that cats rarely meow to each other; a kitten will meow to its mother, but this dies out as it becomes more independent and can use scent and body language to communicate with other cats. Around humans, however, meowing is continued into adulthood as a way to get our attention or make us aware of something, as well as an attempt at something like a conversation.

Sadly, not all cats have a person to talk to; according to some estimates, there are tens of millions of stray and feral cats globally. While many have always lived without human contact, some are escaped or abandoned pets that have quickly reverted to a wilder way of life. Feral kittens can usually be tamed and adopted, but adults distrust humans.

Shelters around the world are inundated with cats and are often unable to find new homes for them, so organisations suggest that all cat owners should have their pets spayed or neutered to avoid adding to the population. Even if a cat is never going to come into contact with another, vets will advise castration because it provides health benefits, such as reducing the risk of certain infections and cancers.

> "IT MAY COME AS A SURPRISE TO LEARN THAT CATS RARELY MEOW TO EACH OTHER. AROUND HUMANS, IT IS A WAY TO GET OUR ATTENTION"

DID YOU KNOW?
A cat lapping at milk is a classic image, but this treat might actually do more harm than good. Once they're weaned, cats don't naturally drink any sort of milk, and cow's milk has much more lactose in it than most cats can process. While some can drink milk occasionally, the best option is a simple bowl of water.

CATS IN CULTURE

Cats have divided opinion since they first strutted into our lives thousands of years ago

TREATED LIKE GODS

In ancient Egypt, cats, known as 'miu', were considered sacred. Dead cats were preserved by mummification and buried with the same respect as humans, and their loss was mourned by their owners.

WITCHES' ACCOMPLICES

In the Middle Ages, cats were thought to be linked to the devil and to act as servants for witches. It was also believed that witches could turn into cats. As a result, cats were feared and often killed.

WEASELLING THEIR WAY IN

Cats didn't play a big role in early Rome or Greece – instead people kept weasels and ferrets as pets and to catch rats. Eventually, cats replaced the mustelids because of their better temperament and efficient hunting.

CHARIOT-PULLERS, CROP PROTECTORS

Freyja, a Norse goddess associated with love, beauty, fertility and war, was said to travel in a chariot pulled by two cats, and farmers would leave out offerings of milk in the hopes that she'd bless their crops.

SYMBOLS OF GOOD LUCK

In Japan, the maneki-neko is a figurine believed to bring good fortune. While it looks like it's waving, it's actually making the Japanese beckoning gesture, so it's especially popular with businesses.

CLOSEST FAMILY
Closely related to the domestic cat are…

WILDCAT
Wildcats occur in Europe, Africa and western and central Asia. There's a large amount of variation across their range, but all wildcats share characteristics with domestic cats, which are derived from the African subspecies Felis silvestris lybica.

SAND CAT
This small cat is the only species able to survive and live in true deserts. With little water to be found in the African and Asian deserts it calls home, the sand cat gets most of the moisture it requires from the prey it consumes, which is mainly rodents.

JUNGLE CAT
The jungle cat, also known as the swamp cat, is the largest living species in the genus Felis. It occupies savannah and forest from Egypt all the way to China, where its strong claws allow it to climb down trees as easily as it climbs up them.

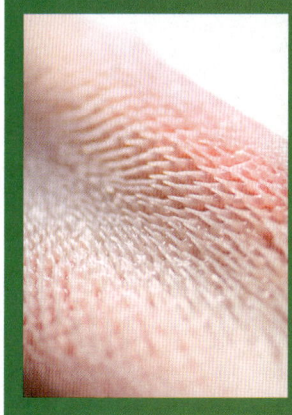

They may be domesticated, but pet cats retain the reflexes they'd have needed to survive in the wild

"IN ANCIENT EGYPT, CATS WERE CONSIDERED SACRED. DEAD CATS WERE PRESERVED BY MUMMIFICATION AND MOURNED BY OWNERS"

SHARP TONGUE

If you've ever had the honour of being licked by a cat, you'll be familiar with the roughness of the feline tongue. It's covered in little barbs, called papillae, that face backwards towards the cat's mouth. They're made of keratin, the same substance as human nails and rhino horns, and they help the cat to clean itself and remove meat from the bones of its prey.

"CONSIDER YOUR HOME — IS IT LARGE ENOUGH FOR A CAT? DO YOU HAVE OUTSIDE SPACE FOR THE CAT TO ROAM? ARE YOU PREPARED FOR ALL THE CAT FLUFF?"

OWNER'S GUIDE: CATS & KITTENS

Get ready fur your new best friend! Here's a purrfect guide to keeping your new moggy as happy as can be

WORDS ELLA CARTER

CHOOSING YOUR NEW CAT

Finding the right feline for you

Cats are amazing companions – they're cute, fluffy, funny and give great cuddles. Everyone should be able to enjoy living with a cat, but before getting your first feline, there are a few things you need to consider.

Up first is the time commitment. Many cats can live to 20 years, so consider your lifestyle and whether you're able to provide for a pet for that long. On a day-to-day basis, although cats don't need your undivided attention, there are a few breeds that don't do well with being left on their own. A Siamese or a Sphynx, for example, would be a better choice for people who are at home more often as they need company. If you're at work all day, consider a more independent breed, such as the British Shorthair or Maine Coon. These felines are quite happy to entertain themselves, but they do have other specific needs to consider, such as grooming. The time commitment is especially true for kittens, which need much more care and attention in their first year of life.

Another point to consider is your home – is it large enough for a cat? Do you have outside space for the cat to roam? Are you prepared for all the cat fluff? Different breeds have different types of fur, but all cats shed, so you'll also need to be prepared to have cat hair in your home. However, that's nothing a good vacuum can't fix. If pet hair is an issue, a 'hypoallergenic' breed might be a good choice for you, such as an Oriental Shorthair or a Rex, as they shed less.

Be honest about if you can meet the financial commitments. You'll need to provide food, cat litter, flea and worm treatment, regular vet care and pay for pet insurance for your cat's entire life.

Although this seems like a lot to consider, as long as you've put the proper thought into owning one, then having a cat is very rewarding and heaps of fun.

TRICKS AND TREATS

The best way to start a relationship with your cat is to enforce good behaviour and forge a strong bond

Many people think that given their independent nature you can't train a cat, but that simply is not true. Although cats don't seem as biddable as dogs, they do respond well to training.

It's best to start training when your cat is young. This will get them used to working with you, although that doesn't mean you can't train older cats as well, it just may take a little more time. Start with the basics of teaching them their name and getting them to come when you call them. The way to do this is the same as with a dog — have something really tasty to hand, reward your cat with plenty of food and give lots of praise when it does what you want it to do. Don't get frustrated if it doesn't do what you want, though. Cats can be perceptive to your mood and just may decide it's not worth it. Use a firm "no" when it does something wrong and then move swiftly on.

Keep your training sessions short, concise and regular; a few minutes every day will pay off. One tip is to do this before mealtimes as this will mean that the cat will be eager for a tasty morsel. However, don't withhold food to make a cat compliant — they'll soon lose interest and wander off to do something else. Ensure that your cat has mastered one skill before moving onto another one, and try not to rush. You need to work as a team and at the same pace.

Treats are a really great way to reinforce your bond with your furry friend as cats are highly motivated by food. The same goes for toys, because cats absolutely love to play and you can experiment to see what your cat enjoys. Through this your cat will associate you with fun and love, which has a great effect on the training as they'll see working with you as an extension of this.

> "TREATS ARE A REALLY GREAT WAY TO REINFORCE YOUR BOND WITH YOUR FURRY FRIEND AS CATS ARE HIGHLY MOTIVATED BY FOOD"

With a bit of dedication your cat can learn to perform all manner of tricks

If you get your cat used to it from a young age, you can take them for walks

CAT-MIN TASKS

Here are some essential tasks to complete, ready for your new cat

PET INSURANCE
This can cost as little as a few pounds a month (in most cases), and should your cat ever need vet treatment, it's certainly well worth having.

TAGGING & CHIPPING
A microchip is essential to make sure your cat can be returned to you if they get lost. In some cases it's free, so ask your vet.

VACCINATIONS
Kittens need to be vaccinated at nine weeks and again at three months. Adult cats then need yearly booster jabs to maintain health.

FLEA & WORM TREATMENT
Keep up with these medications to ensure your cat stays healthy! Lots of vets will offer this on a subscription basis.

SPAYING & NEUTERING
Unless you're looking to breed your pet, always spay or neuter your cat. This can be done at around four months old.

VACCINATION RECORD
Keep your cat's vaccination record safe — you'll need it if you want a pet passport and some catteries require one.

PET TECH

The modern world is all about pets – from Insta-famous kitties to gadgets that make cat care easier. For example, check out the Catit Senses 2.0 Wellness Center, which provides all kinds of elements to keep your cat happy, including a full body massager, dental hygiene and grooming tech. There's a whole host of robotic self-cleaning litter boxes, app-controlled cat toys, treat mazes and puzzles, kitty cameras to make sure your furry friend is okay while you're away, and even automated feeding stations. If that's not enough, perhaps you'd consider investing in the Litter Kwitter, a device that sits over your own toilet seat, designed to eliminate the need for a litter box.

There are even downloadable interactive apps for your tablet that will keep your cat busy

Cats are clever critters – provide plenty of fun by hiding treats in pet puzzles for them to solve

KITTY KIT
These items are vital for making your feline feel at home

BED
Although cats are well known for snoozing in weird spots, it's good to get their own space so they feel safe and secure.

FOOD AND WATER BOWLS
Feeding time is important. Invest in wide and shallow bowls and keep them in one spot so your cat knows exactly where its meals will be.

COLLAR
Be sure to purchase a collar with an elastic loop – this will ensure that your cat can slip out of it should the collar get caught.

SCRATCHING POST
Cats have a natural urge to scratch and almost any surface will do. Make sure to get them a special post in order to protect your furniture.

TRAVEL CRATE
This may not seem essential at first, but if you need to take your cat to the vet in an emergency it's great to have to hand. In fact, some vets insist cats are in a hard crate.

LITTER TRAY
Cats instinctively use litter trays as it means they can cover their waste. Many can be trained to go outdoors, but it's a good backup.

CATS AND THEIR HUMANS

Our feline friends get a rep for being haughty, but most of the time it's simple misunderstandings that come between cats and the owners of their dreams

WORDS ELLA CARTER

What's not to love about a kitty? Big adorable eyes, soft downy fur, adorable purring noises, 'toe beans'? They tick all of the cute, fuzzy boxes that we humans just love. It's no surprise that roughly 27 per cent of households in the UK are home to a cat. But for those who are less feline-inclined, cats have a reputation for being aloof, unfeeling, overtly sassy and just plain mean. But why? Where did cats pick up the reputation for being fluffy jerks, and why is it so unfair?

BACK TO BASICS

The domestication of cats began around 12,000 years ago – when humans started to farm land and stockpile crops. Having wild cats prowl through the grain stores became useful for keeping a pesky rodent population at bay; then the less bitey ones were likely rewarded with extra scraps from the table to entice them to stick around. Fast forward a few thousand years and there's your own kitten, sampling a little taste of tuna from your fork like no time has passed!

Even now, there's very little genetic difference between the wildcat and a common house moggy; they look almost identical. To prevent the primal instincts taking hold, kittens need to meet humans and get used to us at a young age. This is so that they can begin the bonding process as domestic pets, as they still possess everything they need to be able to hunt for themselves and live in the wild without us.

This is definitely the first mark against the good cat name – the fact that they don't really need us to exist. It's a trait that's revered by the cat appreciators (independence is a wonderful pet quality!), but can also be seen as an aloof and even ungrateful attitude from an animal that you dote on. But we're not giving cats the credit they deserve here. They have evolved as solitary hunters that instinctively look out for number one. Dogs, on the other hand, are pack animals that slot in very nicely to the family structure that we adopt ourselves, so it's no wonder that the default cat attitude to keep to themselves appears slightly at odds with our own pack-style family values.

ATTITUDE IS EVERYTHING

That's not to say that cats aren't social – they just do this in their own special way. Studies have shown that cats and kittens form close bonds with their caregivers in a similar way to children and dogs, but strike two comes from the fact that, rather unhelpfully, cats often seem to employ a law of opposites when it comes to affection. For example, staring. This isn't your fluffball fixing you with a rude glare; it's actually cat for "I love you" – if coupled with a slow eye blink, your cat is basically declaring you soulmates. Also, refusing to settle down and spend time with you is not any kind of aloof avoidance or purposeful disruption; instead it's actually your cat exhibiting that they have a secure attachment to you and feel confident and energetic in your presence, resulting in excited exploration.

"THEY HAVE EVOLVED AS SOLITARY HUNTERS THAT INTINCTIVELY LOOK OUT FOR NO.1"

Cats form close bonds with their owners, with similar attachment styles shown in babies and dogs

That said, anyone who has been on the receiving end of an adorable head bump or napped next to the slow rumble of a contented cat purr will easily attest to feeling the love from their kitty in an clear, unmistakable way.

BRINGING THE WILD IN

Hunting is another cat behaviour that doesn't really win them any fans. You feed your kitty all the luxury cat foods out there, and yet they still hunt, eat dead stuff and sometimes bring you 'presents'. How could receiving a gift of mangled animal remains ever be perceived as a kind, friendly gesture?

Cats are natural born carnivores, and while your pet is perfectly aware that their next meal will be supplied by you, the allure of the hunt is still very much hardwired in. It's a fun, thrilling sport to flex their feline muscles, but it's this blood lust that doesn't do much for cats in the public opinion stakes. However, when they bring you these little trophy presents, your cat is actually treating you as their family and helping you to learn to hunt and fend for yourself, just as they'd train kittens in the same way. When you think about it like that, it's actually quite rude to react with revulsion at the dead bird on the doormat!

In the wild, cats will sometimes form social groups in neutral territory and loosely co-exist if there's a regular food source, but as territorial animals, their preference is usually to keep to their home patch. It's this territorial nature that can also contribute to a cat's perceived aloofness – they definitely don't want to come with you on adventures or take a walk (there's that inevitable dog comparison again!). This is because the home they share with you is their safe little world and leaving it would only cause lots of stress and anxiety.

Territorial behaviour is also the reason why cats like to disappear and head off into the night on their own (that, plus the promise of a mouse snack) – again adding to their reputation of being rather unavailable deserters. Patrolling and defending territory comes naturally to them, but the fact that they come back into your house, curl up and snooze the day away is a huge compliment that they feel super at peace in their territorial safe zone.

"CATS ARE GIVEN A BUM DEAL IN COMPARISON TO DOGS"

MAKE NO COMPARISON

First of all – despite the fact that we've been doing it for decades – we probably shouldn't continue to compare cats and dogs. They're just not the same! And as dogs appear to have more traits that us humans instinctively recognise as positive and welcoming, cats are given a bum deal by comparison.

We're also all guilty of projecting our human interpretation of behaviour onto cats, and associate their ways as rude or offensive just as we would do if one of our friends turned their back to us during a conversation, when in reality it's quite the opposite. But if it's hard to separate your human feelings from cat ones, how about this instead: there are some who compare their cats to their human friends. While dogs are biddable and obedient (although a quick hat tip here to the cats who have been trained to use the toilet, no one can say they can't be trained!), cats truly make their own choices. Sometimes they include you, sometimes they don't, in the exact same way that our own human friends are free to govern themselves as they please. Perhaps we've been thinking about our pets all wrong!

If your kitty is staring, don't be alarmed. It's not a challenge or a glare, it's actually true cat love

6 WAYS YOU CAN TELL YOUR CAT LOVES YOU

Contrary to popular opinion, cats can feel love; they just have a unique way of showing it. Here are some examples of how they communicate their affection

WORDS BECKY BRADBURY

1 THEY TREAT YOU LIKE A CAT
Cats who groom each other and sleep side-by-side are very much at ease in each other's company. So when your pet snuggles up nearby for some shut eye or licks you while it's being stroked, it means they trust you too.

2 THEY FOLLOW YOU AROUND
If a cat shadows your every move, it's not just because they're hungry. Most of the time it's a sign you share a close bond. Cats are simply curious about what their person is doing.

3 THEY BLINK AT YOU
Among cats, a prolonged, unblinking stare is a sign of aggression and therefore meant to be intimidating. However, slow, soft blinks signal their intentions aren't hostile – and when directed at humans it's a way of communicating you're their friend. Blink back to let them know the feeling's mutual!

4 THEY KNEAD YOU
A kitten will instinctively knead its mother while feeding to encourage milk flow. When a cat carries this trait into adulthood and does it to you, take it as a compliment. It means they feel happy, safe and comforted in your presence.

5 THEY SHOW YOU THEIR BELLY
The most vulnerable spot for a cat is its stomach, so they only expose it to people they completely trust. But if your cat is displaying their belly, you should still proceed with caution. Many cats aren't comfortable with their tummy being stroked, so might take a swipe at you.

6 THEY BRING YOU GIFTS
Cats adore showing off their prized catches to those they like best. Hence all those dead mice left on your doorstep! These 'presents' are also a cat's attempt at providing for their family, meaning they consider you their next of kin.

HOW SMART ARE CATS?

Our feline friends are often seen, ironically, as the underdogs to their canine counterparts in the brains department. Is it time to reassess what we think we know about the moggy mind?

WORDS ADAM MILLWARD

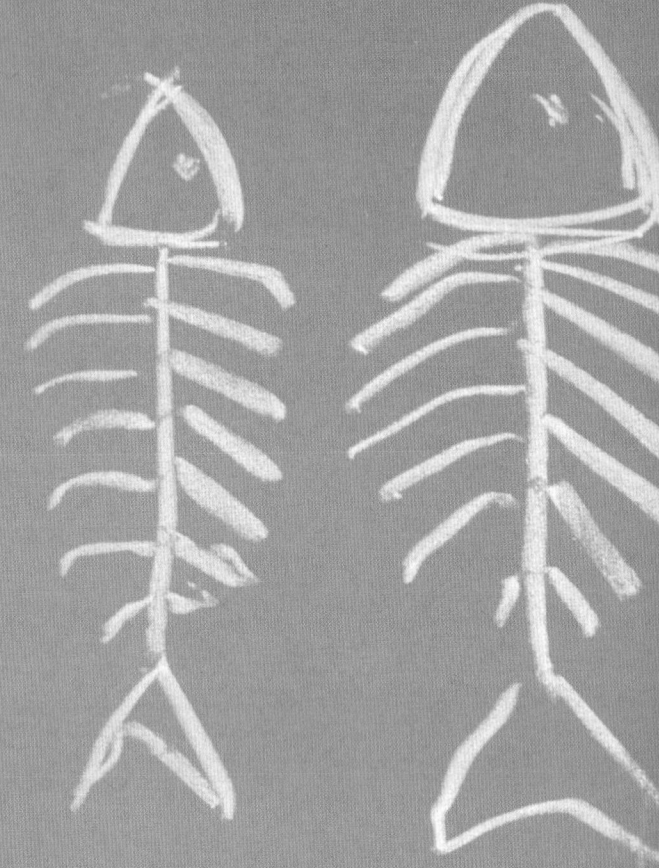

WHICH ARE SMARTER – CATS OR DOGS?

It's one of those contentious debates that elicits impassioned opinion from both sides. Which camp you fall in will depend on your personal experience living with either or both animals, as well as the impressions you subconsciously glean from others.

Before you start to tackle a loaded question like this, it's imperative to recognise some basic truths. Just as with humans, there's no universal method for assessing intelligence – different parameters will wield different results as we will discover in this feature. Also just like people, each pet is an individual that can fall anywhere on a broad spectrum of mental prowess. It would be wrong to lump all cats or all dogs in a binary 'smart' or 'dumb' club, as there will always be exceptions to a rule.

THE PUBLIC PURR-CEPTION

Anyone who has ever seen *Tom & Jerry*, Itchy & Scratchy in *The Simpsons*, or *Sylvester & Tweety* will know that feline characters in kids' shows often fall short of their more diminutive adversaries in a war of wits. Canine personas that appear in such cartoons are typically physically superior, but not intellectually – a triumph more of brawn than brains. In the 2001 movie *Cats & Dogs*, in a fantasy world of pet espionage, cats take the upper paw when it comes to cunning, contrasted to lovable but often blundering Fido foes.

These are, of course, fictional scenarios, but depictions like these set up certain prejudices from a young age, which can be reinforced as we get older. Who hasn't seen a video (or ten if you've fallen down a rabbit hole!) on social media where dogs and cats are presented with a similar challenge – such as a corridor full of objects on the floor that must be navigated – where the light-footed moggy pulls off a flawless manoeuvre whereas the hapless hound's attempt ends in epic calamity?

The odd thing is that this cat-trumps-dog trope runs contrary to the widely established view that dogs are more intellectually

Feline intelligence is a topic that splits the crowd — among pet owners and professional animal behaviourists alike

6 SMARTEST CAT BREEDS

Which types of cat are top of the class?

BENGAL
Descended from Asian leopard cats, this breed retains a wild streak in both looks and character. As well as climbing, they love toys and puzzles and have the dexterity to manipulate small objects and even light switches!

ABYSSINIAN
One of the oldest cat breeds is also considered one of the most intelligent. Abyssinians are extremely inquisitive. They can be taught tricks using a clicker and can even take on agility courses.

CORNISH REX
Sociable, curious and quick to learn – but also with a propensity for mischief! Keep them from getting into trouble by occupying them with trick training and treat-giving puzzles.

SIAMESE
These social cats are not shy about expressing themselves and like to stick close to their owners. They're eminently trainable, open to learning tricks like fetch and even being walked on a leash.

SAVANNAH
Another wild-domestic hybrid (this time descended from the African serval), you'll want to provide plenty of enrichment toys for these energetic mega-moggies or risk them taking out their boredom on the furniture!

SCOTTISH FOLD
The wide-eyed stars of many YouTube videos might look like super cute anime characters but don't let that fool you: they love brain-teasing toys to keep them amused, as well as plenty of human interaction.

Brain size doesn't always correlate to IQ so it would be wrong to rank cats as cognitively inferior due to this

"THE DOMESTIC CAT BRAIN MAKES UP ABOUT 0.9% OF ITS BODY MASS"

gifted because of their aptitude to learn. Whether it's basic tricks like "sit" and "roll over" to more complex feats of agility or vital jobs in the emergency services (such as search and rescue) or as assistant pets, our canine companions excel on virtually all fronts. There's no denying that dogs perform many more interactive roles in society than cats, but are we falling into the trap of equating intelligence with something else?

TESTING PET IQ

So what do the scientists have to say on the matter? Surely they must have reached a verdict on the cat-dog cognitive conundrum by now?

One figure who is often spotlighted in this discussion is the Brazilian neurologist Suzana Herculano-Houzel. She has devised a method of counting the number of neurons in the cerebral cortex — a region linked with higher functions including thought, awareness, language and memory. While initially focusing on the human brain, Dr Herculano-Houzel has applied the same technique to assess those of cats and dogs (a mixed-breed and a Golden Retriever).

When it came to neuron count, the Retriever came out on top with an estimated 627 million neurons in its cerebral cortex; the mixed dog had 429 million; the cat, meanwhile, had 250 million. To give some context, the average human cerebral cortex boasts around 16 billion.

This may seem like an open-shut case, but Dr Herculano-Houzel is the first to highlight her findings don't necessarily resolve this age-old debate. "Neurons are the basic information processing units. The more units you find in the brain, the more cognitively capable the animal is," she explains, but with a proviso: "We definitely need more research on this topic before we can definitively state how meaningful brain size is as a measure of intelligence across different animal groups."

Biologically speaking, felines have proportionally less grey matter, too. The domestic cat brain makes up about 0.9% of its body mass, compared to 1.2% in a dog and 2% in a human. But it would be wrong to assume this immediately ranks cats as cognitively inferior, as size doesn't always correlate to IQ — for instance, several early humans (including Neanderthals) had larger brains than modern Homo sapiens. It's how efficiently a brain works, not its overall size, that determines its efficacy.

Also, while physiology seems to favour dogs, the results of behavioural studies are more complex.

Take the ability to interpret human gestures. Research conducted by Professor Ádám Miklósi, an ethologist at Eötvös Loránd University in Hungary, revealed that cats were pretty much as adept as dogs at what is called the 'pointing test'. This involves a human signalling to an upturned cup (covering a treat) and ignoring other cups that don't hide a treat and seeing how the animal reacts. This would indicate that cats, like dogs, possess 'theory of mind' — the ability to comprehend another animal's thought process, at least to some degree; in this case, "if you follow where I'm pointing, you'll find a tasty snack".

Taking this experiment to the next level, Professor Miklósi placed a bowl of food in a difficult-to-access position and left the subjects to find and extract it. In the first stage, both dogs and cats easily tracked down the food and used their paws to move the bowl. In the second stage, the bowl was fixed in place so it couldn't be retrieved. Typically cats persisted for much longer than dogs in trying to solve this puzzle. Dogs caught on more rapidly that this was an impossible challenge and went to seek help from their owner. You might argue that it's smarter to realise when a task is out of your control and to request assistance, but it does highlight a key characteristic that frequently separates these two much-loved pets: independence.

Dogs appear to possess more quantitative reasoning (an ability to count) than cats but linguistics is a closer contest. In terms of

A study showed that cats respond better to human interaction than toys or food

> "WHILE DOGS MAY BE BETTER LISTENERS, CATS APPEAR TO BE THE SUPERIOR SPEAKERS"

interpreting human language, both animals seem to easily learn their names as well as fundamentals that matter to them most such as "dinner", "good boy/girl" and "no". A large part of this interpretation is achieved through tuning into tone, reading the context and observing body language. A divergence between cats and dogs does emerge in the breadth of vocabulary they can retain. Whereas cat capacity seems to max out at 20-40 words or phrases, for dogs that leaps to 90-100 words on average, and in one exceptional case up to 215 according to research published by Canada's Dalhousie University in 2021. (Incidentally, the top performing breeds were herding dogs, such as Australian Shepherds and Border Collies.)

While dogs may be better listeners, on the flipside, cats (at least colloquially) appear to be the superior speakers, with a vast range of nuanced purrs, meows, hisses, yowls and chirps. Some estimates put their vocal repertoire being as diverse as 100 different vocalisations — significantly more than dogs. Which perhaps begs the question: are we humans actually intelligent enough to understand cats?

In terms of memory, dogs and cats are on a par. If it involves primitive necessities, such as the location of food and water, or recalling something that caused great fear (such as the vacuum cleaner) or, conversely, pleasure (such as remembering the sunniest windowsill), these day-to-day survival skills seem to get hard-baked into both animals' long-term memories. For more trivial non-essentials, such as toys and tricks, it seems to come down to the individual animal — with dogs generally outperforming cats simply because for the most part they seem to derive far more pleasure from play.

All this is to say that even today in the 21st century, the results are far from conclusive. A major stumbling block is that far more

Dogs tend to outperform cats when it comes to tricks, but they get more enjoyment from play

research has been done with dogs than cats — and a key reason for this has nothing to do with understanding or ability, but rather a willingness to participate.

PERSONALITY VS INTELLIGENCE

Now we get to the crux of the dog versus cat intellect debate. Even the staunchest of doggy defenders would have to concede that in the vast majority of traditional intelligence tests, cats are more than capable of holding their own, whether it's in problem solving, memory recall or a propensity to learn and communicate. Where the divide between the two species rapidly opens is when it comes to engagement.

There's a very good reason that we currently have far more knowledge about the inner workings of canine minds... and that's because dogs are by their nature more willing to participate and far more eager to please. Frequently in studies of domestic cats, huge numbers of the sample have to be disregarded simply because they refuse to acknowledge, let alone take part in, a set task. At which point the question becomes not so much 'are cats smart enough to do something' but 'are cats in the mood to do something'?

Cat behaviourist Dr Sarah Ellis points out that we may be starting out with a flawed premise by pitching cats and dogs literally head-to-head. She explains: "I don't think it's fair to compare a cat's intelligence to that of a dog's as they are completely different species and tests for intelligence should be designed specifically to a species' behavioural needs, so ultimately, depending on how a test is designed, one species is going to fare better than the other."

This is something we can rectify, though. A 2017 study from Oregon State University found that cats typically responded much more positively to human interaction than they did food or toys (dogs, of course, respond to all three). Perhaps it is us who need to retrain our brains – as Dr Ellis says, we need to cater intelligence tests to the species being tested, rather than attempt to apply a one-size-fits-all approach.

Another point that must be highlighted is that pooches have a distinct advantage: they have been living with us for far longer. Best guesses vary for when wild wolves first began to integrate with human communities but conservative estimates put it at least 15,000 years ago. More recent studies suggest even longer, perhaps 25,000 years or as much as 40,000 years. Compare that to the earliest known (presumed) domesticated cat on record – a 9,500-year-old moggy found interred with its owner in Cyprus. Even the very earliest dates put forward for when cats were first domesticated are 12,000 years ago.

This could go a long way to explaining that fierce independent streak cats retain – as well as wild instincts such as their hunting ability – compared to far-more dependent dogs. In the battle of 'street smarts' and being able to take care of themselves, cats almost always come out on top. And who is to say that survivor skills aren't the ultimate test of intelligence, far more important than how many tricks you can perform?

As a sidenote, it's a total myth that cats are incapable of being trained or doing tricks. Admittedly, some cat breeds seem to be more amenable to learning than others (see side panel) but don't write off any moggy before giving it a go. If you want inspiration, Anika Moritz from Austria set a world record with her tortoiseshell tabby Alexis in 2020. The pair rattled through 26 different tricks in one minute, ranging from waving and high fives to ringing a bell and touching her nose.

Given humans and dogs have had so many more millennia to get to know one another's social interactions and thought processes, who knows what the human-cat relationship will look like in another 10,000 or so years? Perhaps by then we will have evolved to another level of understanding, at which point the pet intellect debate as it stands now could be turned on its head.

By the same token, we could give it another 100,000 years and cats could be just as single-minded, only willing to play ball (sometimes literally) if and when they feel like it. For now, we'll have to console ourselves with the fact that while dogs are the consummate teachers' pets, always eager to show off their knowledge, our feline friends are the reluctant straight-A students that are too cool for school.

Q&A

WITH DR SARAH ELLIS

Dr Sarah Ellis is the head of cat advocacy at International Cat Care, co-author of *The Trainable Cat* (2016) and expert on BBC TV series *Cat Watch*

DO YOU THINK CAT INTELLIGENCE IS MISUNDERSTOOD?

I think some people take a cat's lesser need for social behaviour in comparison to other species, such as dogs, as a lesser intelligence, but intelligence is so much more than just ability to navigate social relationships.

CAN CATS BE TAUGHT TRICKS?

Yes, they learn really well with positive reinforcement, but the question I would ask is why teach them tricks when you can teach them useful things such as to come when called, to feel content in the cat carrier, or be comfortable with handling and medications – these are skills for life.

ARE THERE WAYS TO ASSESS CAT INTELLIGENCE? WHAT ABOUT WAYS TO BOOST IT?

There are lots of ways to assess intelligence and many scientists have been devising studies to do just that, for example, some include finding food while others involve trying to mentally match sounds to pictures or solve difficult tasks. Giving your cat an enriched and stimulating home environment is the best way to exercise their brains – lots of places to explore and climb, puzzle feeders to hunt out food and lots of play where they have to use their mental and physical skill to catch a toy.

ARE CERTAIN CAT BREEDS PRONE TO BEING SMARTER THAN OTHERS?

There is probably as much individual variation in intelligence between individual moggies as there are between breeds. However, some breeds have been bred to have specific characteristics. So, for example, if the intelligence test involves vocalisations, vocal cats such as Siamese and Orientals may fare better. However, that doesn't mean overall they are more intelligent. I think any cat lover will tell you that when it comes to cats – an animal that has evolved from one that can survive without help from any others – every individual cat shares that intelligence.

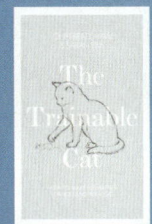

The Trainable Cat is available for £9.99 from Penguin Books

CAT CHAT

How to decode the hidden messages within our moggies' surprisingly varied vocabulary

WORDS ADAM MILLWARD

From an early age, we learn that cats "meow" to communicate. It's as fundamental as a dog's "woof", a cow's "moo" or a horse's "neigh". But for anyone that has ever been a cat owner – or indeed interacted with any of these animals – you'll know that's drastically oversimplifying. Our feline friends, in particular, have developed a plethora of ways to tell us their desires and feelings.

There are colloquial reports that domestic cats have as many as 100 different vocalisations in their repertoire. A more conservative – but nevertheless still impressive – 21 vocalisations are laid out in a study that was published in the *Journal of Veterinary Science* in 2020.

These include familiar favourites such as meowing and purring, but also a few you might typically associate with other species altogether, including squeaks, chirrups and growls.

Not all vocalisations are used by all cats, of course, so don't worry if your moggy seems to be keeping schtum on you. Some vocal expressions are reserved for interaction with humans, others for talking to fellow felines and others still for engaging with other animals. To get you on the road to speaking fluent feline, get to grips with these six common vocalisations.

LEARNING TO SPEAK FE-LINGO

1 MEOW
It's the most famous cat chat of them all – but what does it mean? Generally used for cat-human communication, the multipurpose meow crops up in many different situations as a way of drawing attention or to request something. The only real way to interpret its particular message is context. Depending on the location and time of day, the same meow could mean "get up", "welcome home", "feed me" or "open the door". Frequency, pitch and length can be useful indicators of different meanings. Quick-fire meows imply a greater sense of urgency; more guttural, drawn-out meowwws can be a sign of anxiety or complaint; higher-pitched, short roooww sounds could imply they're ticked off and not in the mood to socialise.

2 PURR
If you asked someone to sum up contentment in a noise, it would most likely be a cat's purr. The throaty murmur that sounds like a humming motor seems to be spontaneously triggered when they are in their happy place, whether that's in your lap being petted, playing with their favourite toy or waiting to be fed. Occasionally this expression can mean quite the opposite, though. Some cats purr when in particularly stressful situations – such as in a vet's waiting room. It's easy to tell the difference between a content purr and a worried purr by observing tell-tale signals that go with it, such as a tense body posture, tail flicking and panting.

3 HISS AND SNARL
Whether you're a human, dog or another cat, you'd have to be pretty tone-deaf to misinterpret what this vocalisation means: "you're scaring and/or annoying me – keep back or else!". Hisses, snarls and growls are almost always used in tandem with visual clues that also kick in when a cat enters survivor mode, such as an arched back, pinned-back ears, bared teeth, fur on end and a twitching tail. Vocal expressions like these are the final warning before a cat resorts to more drastic measures such as scratching or biting. The best response is to give your pet plenty of space and seek to calm them by getting rid of the thing (whether it's a person, an animal or an object) that provoked this reaction.

4 YOWL AND SCREAM
A yowl is a longer-lasting, more heartfelt meow usually reserved for communicating with other cats. It's most commonly used as a warning in territorial disputes, perhaps with neighbours they don't get on with, or conversely while on the hunt for a mate, perhaps with neighbours that they get on with very well. For females in heat, this call is sometimes referred to as a caterwaul. If your cat begins to yowl or scream a lot at home, something isn't right. They might just be feeling restless, in which case some supportive strokes or playing with a favourite toy could put their mind at ease. Worst-case scenario, they may be telling you they're not well, in which case get them checked out.

5 CHIRP, CHATTER AND TRILL
Attentive owners will notice that our feline friends produce a range of more subtle vocalisations that can reveal their state of mind – both positive and negative. Chirps, tweets and trills are often a form of greeting, or may be employed to rally other cats they live with, or when their curiosity has been piqued (eg, "did I just hear the treat cupboard open?"). On the other hand, it might be a way of expressing disgruntlement or that something unexpected has startled them. Some moggies will express frustration by "chattering" – the human equivalent of teeth grinding – most often when they can see something they want, like a bird in the garden, that is out of their reach.

> "OUR FELINE FRIENDS HAVE DEVELOPED A PLETHORA OF WAYS TO TELL US THEIR FEELINGS"

Context is king: the trick to speaking 'cat' is a holistic approach, assessing not just the sound, but the time, place and accompanying body language

Just as with humans, sometimes a cat's involuntary physical reactions can reveal far more about what they're thinking and feeling than what they say vocally

CAT BODY LANGUAGE

Our feline friends have far more to say than "meow" – but sometimes the best way to understand them is to listen with our eyes

WORDS ADAM MILLWARD

Not all will admit to it, but pet owners are notorious for anthropomorphizing. We just can't seem to help projecting our human behaviours and feelings onto domesticated species like cats.

One area where this becomes apparent is communication: an assumption that cats only express themselves vocally. While, of course, vocalisations do play a part in inferring our moggies' needs and desires, cats tell us things all the time – often without ever opening their mouths. Sometimes body language can be blatant and sometimes it can be subtle. In either case, the onus is on us to acquaint ourselves with these signals, and pay close attention to how and when they are used by our individual animals. Trying to imagine the world from your cat's perspective is pivotal to success.

Be warned: physical cues don't always equate to the same feeling, so never assume your cat's mood, even from what might seem a tell-tale clue. Assess their body as a whole, read the location and situation, think how would this make you feel. Take the time to observe as well as to listen, and the bond between you and your feline companion will become stronger than ever.

"CATS TELL US THINGS ALL THE TIME – OFTEN WITHOUT OPENING THEIR MOUTHS"

WHY CATS LICK

Cats are consummate groomers, taught to do so by their mother as kittens. To perform this job, they are equipped with a tongue covered in lots of backward-facing barbs – hence its distinct rough texture! The jury's out as to whether they are attempting to clean us when they occasionally give us a lick. More likely, it's a sign of affection, seeking to reinforce social bonds, as they would with other cats. Alternatively – less heartwarmingly – some cat behaviourists believe it's a way of marking their territory (similar to cheek rubbing), letting others know you're their human.

TAILS OF THE UNEXPECTED

Easy to overlook, these agile appendages can be extremely revealing – if you know what to look for...

Everyone knows that you can tell a lot about a dog's mood from its tail. But did you know that feline tails are even more expressive than their canine counterparts? In fact, it can be argued that cats use their tails to talk more than any other part of their body.

First, it can act as a semaphore. Cats are able to manipulate their tails into all manner of shapes and positions so at a quick glance, other cats – and with time humans too – can gauge their state of mind from a distance. Different tail positions reveal whether your moggy is feeling sociable, confident and playful, or at the other end of the spectrum, fretful, frustrated and would rather be left alone.

If the initial static tail position doesn't get their message across, cats can hammer it home by introducing some motion. Twitches, swishes and flicks are all useful mood indicators – sometimes a final warning before they revert to a more claws-on approach!

Part of the spine, the tail and where it joins the body are packed with nerve endings and super sensitive, so for many moggies, they don't like to be overly petted in this area. Part of that may also be because, by interfering with the tail, you're depriving them of a vital part of their communication toolset. So it's important to bear this in mind when you (or especially young children) are interacting with your pet.

As with any body language, it's important to take 'tail talk' in tandem with what the rest of the body is doing and the situation at hand. This is because some signals can mean more than one thing, which are best not mixed up; for instance, cat tails can point upwards when they are both in the mood for some attention and when they are spoiling for a fight!

"FELINE TAILS ARE EVEN MORE EXPRESSIVE THAN THEIR CANINE COUNTERPARTS"

Tail position and movements can offer some useful insights into feline feelings, though be mindful that some can present mixed messages!

10 TYPES OF TAIL TALK

STRAIGHT-UP
A tail standing straight up could indicate a confident, friendly cat open to socialising. If the end is slightly hooked, they may be a little wary or undecided, but are still curious.

HANGING-LOW
If the tail is held straight down or close to the back legs, the cat is likely feeling alert or on edge and is currently assessing a situation, trying to determine what action to take next.

WRAPPED AROUND
Using the tail as a barrier can be a defensive posture when awake; when asleep it acts more as a 'do not disturb' sign. Of course, if it's cold, it's a useful blanket, too.

SWISHING
Whereas dogs wag their tails when happy, the slower swish of a cat's tail typically denotes mild irritation. It can also be a form of acknowledgement if you've called their name and they're asleep but can't be bothered to get up.

TWITCHING
Cats often twitch their tails when on high alert, especially when hunting or playing. It can suggest annoyance, so approach with care and keep hands at a distance.

BRISTLING
An erect tail can indicate a combative mood, particularly if it looks bushier than normal. When scared or territorial, a cat's fur will stand on end to make themselves look bigger – an evolutionary tactic called piloerection.

THUMPING
If your moggy is thumping its tail on the ground while seated or lying down, it's likely angry or overstimulated – best to give it a wide berth!

TUCKED-LEGS
Also like dogs, a tail tucked between the back legs is a sure-fire sign of unease and/or submission. Give them some space and speak in soft tones to reassure them.

SLIGHT-DROOP
As a rule of thumb, the further away the tail is from the body, the more relaxed a moggy is, as signalled by a raised but slightly drooping tail, in line with the spine.

QUIVERING
Sometimes your cat is so excited to see you (or get their dinner), the tip of their tail will literally quiver with anticipation. It's the equivalent of a dog's wag.

FELINE FACETIME

They say the eyes are the window to the soul, but they're not the only facial features with secrets to tell

Among humans, the face is the nexus of social interaction. As well as the all-important mouth and eyes through which we directly exchange speech and looks, more involuntary reactions such as a wrinkled brow, a yawn or raised eyebrows help us to perceive others' thoughts and navigate through a conversation.

It's natural, therefore, that we should instinctively place equally high significance on our cats' faces as well. While it's certainly important to remember that cats use their whole bodies to communicate, that's not to say there isn't a lot to be gleaned from feline facial cues.

When observing a cat's head for clues of what's going on inside it, there are some key signals to focus on. Looking at the eyes first, how open are they, where are they looking and how dilated are the pupils? For the ears, which direction(s) are they facing and how are they positioned compared to normal? Even what might seem like static features, such as the whiskers, can reposition themselves – generally, whiskers angled forward means alert or excited, pressed back means frightened or angry. Less cryptic facial reactions such as snarling and bared teeth should hopefully need no decoding!

The trick is weighing up what your cat's face is telling you in conjunction with what the rest of their body is doing – and of course not to forget any accompanying vocalisations. All-round cat comms will always be more than the sum of its parts.

Facial features such as eyes, ears and whiskers can all be useful barometers of your moggy's mood – especially when taken in context with other signs

HEADS UP!

What are your cat's eyes, ears and whiskers telling you?

RELAXED
When content and relaxed, the head stands proud above the body and moves freely to better follow what is going on around. Eyes are semi-open to closed, while ears and whiskers are at rest in their default positions.

ANXIOUS
As nerves ramp up, the head moves lower so it's in line with the back. Ears start to flatten and may point out sideways; the pupils are virtually fully dilated as fight-or-flight instinct kicks in.

ALERT
When something piques your cat's interest, the eyes open more fully. Ears may swivel towards the object or person that has caught their attention as they seek more information in order to review the situation.

TENSE
If starting to get tense, the head tends to draw back into the chest. The pupils are semi-dilated and the eyes may dart around, looking for possible escape routes. Ears reorient, sometimes in different directions.

SCARED
When truly scared, the cat's head moves below the rest of the body. Ears bend back almost flat to the head and even whiskers reorient backwards. These warnings typically go hand-in-hand with snarling and hissing.

STRIKE A POSE

Sometimes it's not about focusing on a single area or feature but observing your cat's entire body shape

Certain parts of a cat are more expressive than others, but it would be a mistake to fixate on these in isolation. Indeed, the reason why cat communication is among the most complex of any domestic animal is that they use their entire bodies to try and get their point across.

Certain postures, like the infamous arched back, indicate very specific emotions but there are some more general rules of thumb that are useful to look out for.

First, which direction is your cat's body pointing? If facing you head on or moving towards you, this suggests they're in a confident mood and receptive to engaging. If they are standing side on, meanwhile, this is a natural fight-or-flight pose, readying themselves to make a getaway, implying they are feeling on edge.

A similar logic applies to how open or closed your cat's posture is. A moggy sprawled out on its side with its legs akimbo and tail stretched out is the epitome of chilled out; contrast that to a cat tightly huddled in a ball with all its paws hidden and tail wrapped around as a shield. This latter cat has resumed a defensive position and is preparing to spring into action.

There are exceptions to the rule – most notably what has come to be called the 'Venus cat trap'. It's something that every cat owner will have fallen for at least once: a cat lying on its back as if inviting a belly rub, then when you go to oblige, your hand falls victim to a vicious onslaught of claws and teeth. What had looked like a playful pose at face value was, in fact, a passive-aggressive self-defence strategy. This common misinterpretation is painful proof of the need to always respect your cat's personal space and never presume you'll always know what's going on in your pet's mind.

There's a good reason there are so many memes about cats defying the laws of physics – but as well as getting into some unlikely tight spots, their flexibility also enables them to express themselves through posture

CONTORTING CONVERSATION

Read your cat's posture for a better clue to their mood

RELAXED
Relaxed cats will lie on their side, with legs and tail splayed out — just be wary about tickling their belly if they're lying on their back as this may be a trap! Standing, a content cat will have straight legs fully extended and the tail will be raised.

ALERT
Responding to a stimulus, the cat will move from their side to lying on their belly or sitting up. The legs have reoriented so all four paws are now in contact with the floor. The tail may begin to twitch.

ANXIOUS
If concern sets in, moggies will get to their feet in preparation to flee. The rear end may be stooped and the tail hanging low and close to the body, with the tip moving erratically, indicative of their restlessness.

FRIGHTENED
If anxiety ramps up, cats assume a tight, ball-like posture with all their feet positioned beneath the body. They remain very still but may begin to visibly shake. Protracted meows or yowls are common at this point.

TERRIFIED
When really scared, the back lifts and the fur on the upper body stands on end to make the cat look bigger. The entire body appears rigid and respiration is fast. Expect hisses and paw swipes for those that venture too close.

WHY DOES MY CAT DO THAT?

No longer will your cat's antics cause you to scratch your head in confusion. Read on to uncover the mystery meanings behind your feline friend's strangest behaviours

Domestic cats have always carried themselves with an air of mystery, and have long been admired for their beauty, grace, and fantastic hunting skills. Scientists believe that the domestication of cats began over 10,000 years ago in the Middle East, but despite this long and storied association with each other, there's still so much for us humans to learn and discover about them. It can be hard for us to know whether our cats are acting on instinct or acting intentionally, and what they are trying to communicate to us with sounds and body language. Even long-time cat owners need to read up on what counts as normal cat behaviour. Over the next few pages, you will discover some of the strangest and most enigmatic things cats do and, most importantly, what they are trying to tell you.

"IT CAN BE HARD TO KNOW WHETHER CATS ARE ACTING ON INSTINCT OR INTENTIONALLY"

Try all you like but we don't think you'll be able to read your cat's mind, even after a good hard stare at each other

> The domestic house cat population could be as large as between 200 and 600 million.

> It doesn't matter if you have work to do – this could be the perfect napping spot

SIT ON MY LAPTOP

Is your cat demanding attention or have they found a nice warm seat?

If you're a cat owner and you like to browse the internet on your laptop, then there is a high chance that you've been interrupted by your cat butting in and blocking your view. Perhaps they've even interrupted a video call or two! While keyboards can make a nice warm place on which to rest, it isn't likely to be the main reason your cat starts pressing keys. Cats have an incredible sense of smell and a very possessive nature, so what is probably happening is that your cat is marking your property with their scent and claiming ownership over it for themselves! It does your cat no harm to gently move them off when necessary.

RUB AGAINST MY LEGS

Is your cat just showing that they are happy to see you, or is there another motivation at play?

When you come home from a day at work or school, does your cat come to greet you at the door and rub their head and body against your legs? It's a trip hazard that every cat owner has to cope with. Rubbing against people and objects is a sign of affection. Cats have scent glands in their cheeks that secrete a pheromone (a chemical that acts like a hormone but outside of the body), which can communicate many different meanings. The act of rubbing glands transfers your cat's scent onto you, erasing other scents you may have gathered throughout the day and marking you as one of their family. It's a territorial behaviour that makes your relationship known to other cats and animals. With many cats this behaviour is also a simple and straightforward request for pets, play, or attention – so reach down and give in to their demands.

A healthy adult cat can jump an average of five or six times its height.

Have the lint roller on standby because your clothes are about to be covered in cat hair

SLEEP A LOT

Cats and kittens look adorable while they sleep – but why do they sleep so much?

There's no need to worry if your cat is sleeping for 15 hours a day – that's just the average! Kittens and elderly cats may sleep up to 20 hours in a 24-hour period. This need for sleep stems from the wild origins of their ancestors. It takes a lot of energy for a wild cat to hunt and catch prey, and to keep their bodies warm. Sleeping conserves all the energy needed for these important tasks and this behaviour is hardwired into your cat, even if they're an indoor cat! Cats will also sleep when they're bored, so always make sure your cat has enough stimulation for its waking hours.

Live with a cat and you will never have your bed to yourself again

STARE AT ME
Your cat's hard gaze may be off-putting, but they're trying to get your attention for a reason

That intense stare your cat directs your way is not an invitation to a staring contest, it's actually just another form of feline communication, though our understanding of it might be incomplete. It could be the sign of a strong bond between you and your cat, as they are less likely to hold eye contact with strangers. It could also be regular curiosity – maybe you're dressed differently or doing something novel. If you have a tendency to give your cat treats or positive attention when you notice them staring at you, then you may have inadvertently trained them to associate staring with a tasty reward or a scratch behind the ears.

Your cat has a special organ that allows them to pick up scents. This is why you may catch them staring into the distance with their mouths open

GET THE ZOOMIES
Are you wondering why it is your cat is racing all around the house?

Did you know that 'the zoomies' has an official, scientific name? It's called 'frenetic random activity periods' and it refers to short bursts of energy displayed by our cats and dogs. The sudden laps around the house or zipping between pieces of furniture tend to be followed by a period of quiet, with the zoomies ending almost as quickly as they began. Though it may cause you some surprise there is no need to feel any alarm, as this is normal behaviour for cats. We know that our cats sleep a lot, so it shouldn't come as a shock that they often have excess energy to burn off! However, it is important that your cat gets enough exercise and enrichment during the day, so do make sure that you're engaging them in active play, such as toys that simulate hunting or boredom-busting puzzles.

The average top running speed for a house cat is 20-30 miles per hour, depending on health, age, and breed.

If you don't have an outdoor cat, you might consider an outdoor enclosure or indoor garden for your cat

Cats may also knead as a way of marking their territory

KNEAD WITH PAWS

Could your cat be an aspiring baker, or perhaps a would-be mime?

Commonly known as 'making biscuits' in corners of the internet, the instinctual behaviour of kneading – when a cat rhythmically pushes their front paws back and forth on a soft surface, such as a blanket or even your stomach – is totally natural. The wild ancestors of cats did this to get comfortable before sleeping, and in house cats it's a sign of happiness and relaxation. It's also a throwback to their kitten years, as suckling kittens will instinctively knead their mother to encourage milk flow. Your relaxed cat is reminded of being warm and safe and having a belly full of milk. If your cat likes to knead you but you find their claws sharp or painful, try to prepare for some quality snuggle time with a blanket barrier. Never trim a cat's claws just because you find them sharp – you should only trim them if they are too long. Talk to your vet if you are unsure.

Just like humans, kittens will lose their temporary kitten teeth and grow permanent adult teeth.

EAT GRASS
If your cat eats grass it could be a sign that they are feeling unwell

Cats are obligate carnivores, which means that they must eat meat to survive. This is due to their need for high levels of protein (and other nutrients) in their diet. However, that doesn't mean that your cat won't crave some greens once in a while – many cat owners report seeing their cat eat grass. There are many different theories as to why cats do this, and none of them relate to taste. It is most likely that small amounts of grasses have different health benefits. Some grasses may work as a laxative to help digestion, others may induce vomiting, which can help a cat get rid of indigestible fur and empty their stomachs of harmful parasites. It's definitely worth buying some cat grass seed to plant outside or to grow indoors.

Cat grass can be grown at home and is another source of enrichment

STRANGER THINGS

Learn how to decode all of your cat's weird and wonderful behaviours

ELEVATOR BUTT

The position of head and front paws down, tail and butt in the air (sometimes called 'elevator butt') has a few different meanings and is known as lordosis. Between cats it can be a romantic invitation, but if performed by your cat to you it's often an invitation for play or a good scratch at the base of their tail.

SUCK WOOL

Cats suck on wool blankets for the same reason a toddler sucks on their thumb – for comfort. The warmth and softness reminds them of suckling from their mother as a kitten. It could be a sign of stress or anxiety, so check your household for changes that might have upset your cat.

DRINK FROM THE TAP

Cats are tempted by the sounds of water running from a tap because their hearing is much better than their eyesight, so the water source is much easier for them to identify. If you're worried that your cat isn't drinking enough, it could be worth investing in a water fountain designed for cats.

STEAL THINGS

Do you lose socks or hair ties more often than your cat-less friends? Cats with a strong hunting instinct will often substitute real prey for little toys or items in your household and in the process, move things around. This behaviour could also be a ploy to get your attention.

LOVE TIGHT SPACES

Cats seek out and rest in tight spaces for the same reasons we humans like a cosy spot – it feels safe. In the wilderness, a wide open plain could make a wild cat more vulnerable to predators, so a hiding place like a box feels secure.

HOW TO STROKE YOUR CAT

Petting can be a wonderful way of building an even stronger bond with your cat – just make sure you're doing it right

WORDS BECKY BRADBURY

Cats are inherently solitary creatures, so their reputation for being detached isn't entirely unfounded. But it doesn't mean your feline friend can't be affectionate. In fact, research suggests cats do like being petted – just on their own terms!

Many animal behaviourists believe cats love being stroked because the motion reminds them of their mother licking and grooming them as kittens. These memories make a cat feel safe and secure.

Another theory is that when cats live together in the wild, they nuzzle and rub up against each other to create a group scent. The pheromones they release are thought to spread between cats and humans too, meaning petting your cat can also provide it with a sense of belonging.

Whatever the reason, stroking your cat will strengthen the bond between you. There is a right and wrong way however, so pay attention to our six steps and learn how to do it properly.

SIGNS OF ENJOYMENT

- PURRING AND EVEN DRIBBLING
- RELAXED POSTURE AND FACIAL EXPRESSION
- KNEADING WITH THEIR FRONT PAWS
- BUNTING – GENTLY BUMPING THEIR HEAD ON YOU
- EARS POINTED UPWARDS AND FORWARDS

1 INTRODUCE YOURSELF

Skipping straight to the stroking stage is bound to make a cat feel threatened. To avoid any potential upset, take the time to introduce yourself, especially if you've never met the cat before. Start by slowly getting down onto their level – crouching or sitting will do. Then gently extend your fingers for them to sniff. Don't invade their space, but stay still and let them come to you. Research shows an interaction lasts longer when the cat, not the human, initiates contact.

2 BEWARE OF BODY LANGUAGE

Pay attention to your movements, as anything too abrupt might startle a cat. Avoid loud, sudden noises as well. It's also very important to be aware of the cat's body language. Signs your advances are unwelcome include a thumping tail, pinned back ears and running away (don't chase them!). If a cat is keen to be stroked, it's likely to rub their cheek against your fingers or nuzzle their head against your hand. Again, let the cat take the lead.

---

① Most cats adore being scratched under the chin and behind the ears, as this is where their scent glands are.

② Beware – the base of the tail has a lot of nerve endings. While some cats love being stroked here, others hate it.

③ A cat's belly is its most vulnerable body part and best avoided, especially if you don't know the animal.

④ Paws and whiskers are two other no-go petting zones, as they're extremely sensitive areas.

⑤ Try gently stroking along the back, from head to tail, with consistent pressure.

3 LEARN WHERE YOUR CAT LIKES TO BE STROKED…

Once you're certain your cat wants to be stroked, take time discovering what it likes. Cats are generally responsive to areas where their scent glands are. These include under the chin, around the cheeks and behind the ears. When petting your cat, it might bump its head against you. Known as bunting, this is your cat's way of marking you as its own – and most cats love to do it. You can then move onto a full body stroke, from the crown to the base of its tail.

4 …AND WHERE IT DOESN'T

Another sweet spot is the supracaudal gland at the base of a cat's tail. While some enjoy being stroked here, others can't stand it or quickly become overstimulated, causing them to lash out. More consistent no-go areas include legs, paws, whiskers and the stomach. When a cat rolls over, it's not an invitation to tickle their tummy, but a sign they're comfortable in your company. Most aren't keen on belly rubs, as it's their most vulnerable body part.

5 GO THE RIGHT WAY

Be sure to give your cat soft, gentle strokes that move in the same direction as their fur grows. This is rather than using a back-and-forth motion. As for the pressure, all cats will have a different preference. The secret here is to always err on the side of caution and start as softly as possible. You'll then be able to gradually build up the pressure. Remain consistent and you'll soon get to know what it is your cat likes best.

6 KNOW WHEN TO STOP

When engaged in a stroking session, it's worth pausing every five seconds or so to 'check in' with your cat. If they continue to rub against you, it's safe to continue but, if not, it might be worth taking a break. Also back off if a cat stops purring, gets up or changes position – this is a sign they've had enough. Respect your cat's choice, as this will reinforce that petting is a good thing and they will keep coming back for more.

SIGNS OF DISLIKE

- BATTING YOUR HAND AWAY WITH THEIR PAW
- THUMPING THEIR TAIL
- HISSING, GROWLING OR BITING
- QUICKLY TURNING THEIR FACE TOWARDS YOU
- EARS LYING FLAT AGAINST THEIR HEAD

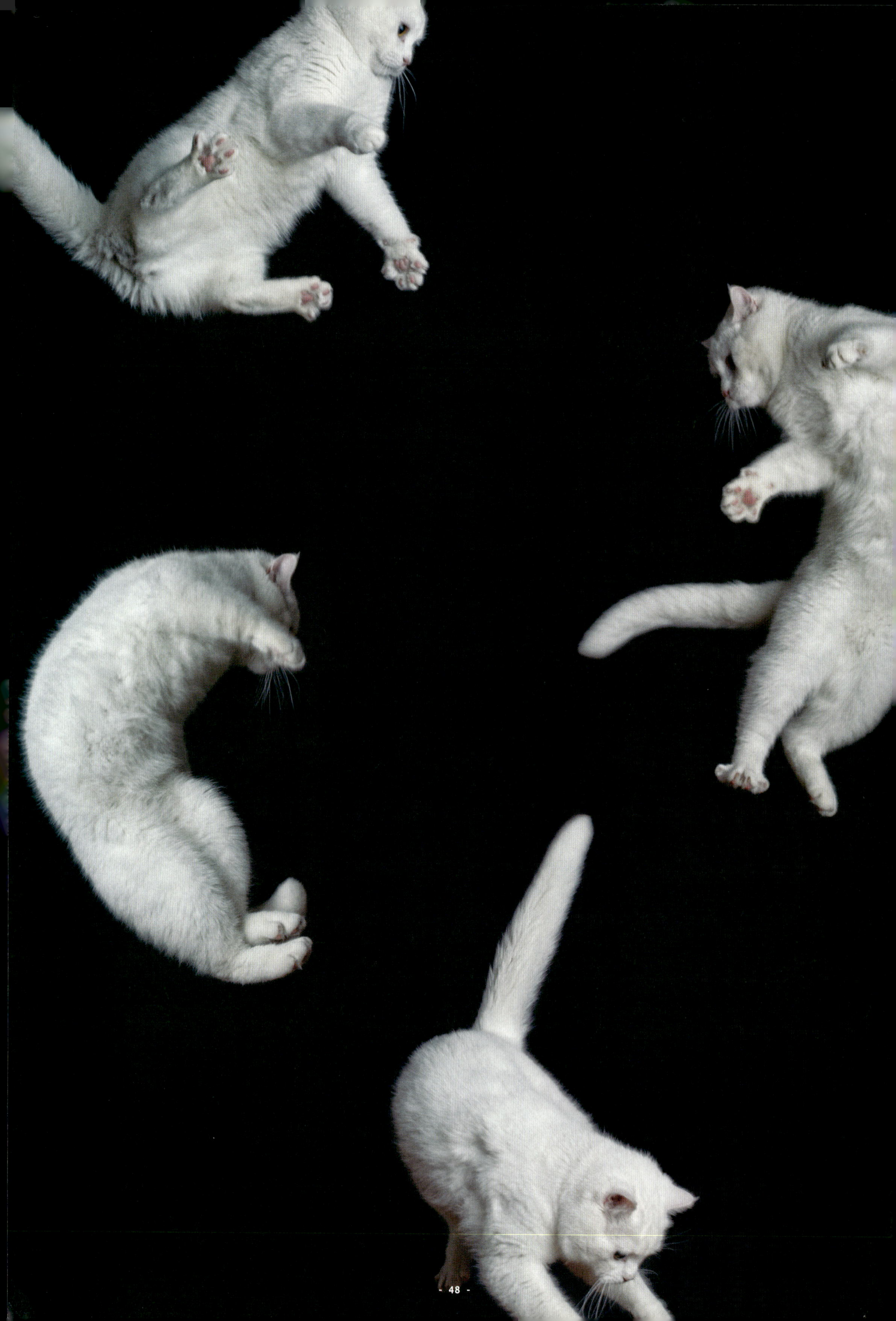

AMAZING ACRO-CATS

Understand how your cat moves so you can cater to their natural instincts

WORDS JO STASS

Whether they're effortlessly climbing the neighbour's fence, gracefully leaping onto their favourite snoozing spot, or playfully pouncing on an unsuspecting toy, our pet moggies are true masters of acrobatic skill. Their sleek, flexible bodies can navigate around most obstacles with ease, and their superb balance helps them to reach impressive heights with expert coordination. If they do happen to fall, they usually have no trouble achieving the purrfect landing, managing to right themselves in mid-air so that all four paws end up on the ground. Many of these skills help with one of their favourite pastimes: hunting. In the wild, cats must hunt prey to survive, but even though our pet cats are usually well-fed from a bowl, they still like to stalk and pounce for enjoyment. Plus, with moggy obesity on the rise, it's important for them to flex their feline muscles and burn off some of those treats.

CAPABLE CLIMBERS

Cats love to climb up high, and the reason why is in their ancestry. Our pet moggies are descended from the African wildcat, which has many predators in the wild. When faced with one of these predators, wildcats will usually try to run away and hide rather than fight and risk injury. The best place for them to run to is usually up a tall tree, and so they use their strong back legs and sharp claws to propel themselves upwards. When they are up high, they also have a great vantage point for surveying their territory, which helps them to spot predators as well as prey.

Although our pet cats don't really have any predators, they still have this natural instinct to run away and get up high if they feel scared, which is why you might sometimes find them on top of a wardrobe or up a tree. The reason many cats struggle to get back down again is because they're not really built for climbing down. Their curved claws and weaker front legs mean they would need to descend backwards, which is not instinctive for a cat. They would much rather jump down, but if they find themselves too high off the ground, they'll be reluctant to risk leaping.

If possible, give your cat somewhere to perch, like their own shelf or buy a climbing tower specially designed for cats. Just make sure they can jump down!

Cats will sometimes chase prey up a tree, then realise they can't get down

WONDER WHISKERS

When sneaking into the neighbour's garden, cats have an amazing ability to fit through the tiniest of gaps in fences and hedges, but how do they know that they won't get stuck? It's all down to their whiskers. These flexible hairs that stick out from their faces are incredibly sensitive, which is why you should use wide, shallow bowls for food and water, and never pull or play with them. They also happen to be roughly the same width as the cat's body. Therefore, before they attempt to squeeze through a small gap, a cat will usually poke their head through to feel the width of the opening with their whiskers. If they don't feel too much pressure on these hairs, then they will judge the gap to be wide enough to fit through.

A cat's ability to fit through these small spaces is largely down to the fact that they don't have a rigid collarbone like we do. Once their head is through the gap, their sleek bodies can slink through without a problem. Of course, some cats do find themselves stuck in various nooks and crannies, and this is usually because they're a little wider than their whiskers would have them believe. When a cat puts on weight, the length of their whiskers doesn't adjust for their expanding waistline, so although their head can fit through a gap, the rest of their body can't necessarily follow with such ease.

A cat's whiskers help them sense whether or not a gap is wide enough to fit through

STEALTHY STALKING AND PERFECTING THE POUNCE

Cats are natural hunters, because in the wild they would need to catch prey in order to survive. Even though our pet moggies usually have their food caught and prepared for them, they still like to stalk and pounce on anything that moves, whether it's their favourite toy or their owner's toes underneath the duvet. This is because the act of catching and 'killing' an object causes the release of happy hormones, called endorphins, in their brain, making them feel content. It's also a great form of exercise, helping them to stay fit and healthy.

When stalking, cats will usually get as low to the ground as possible, as this helps them to sneak up on their prey – or toy – undetected. They may then start to wiggle their backsides, which is their way of testing the stability of the ground before they spring into action. It may also help to warm up their leg muscles before they leap. When they're happy that they have a stable surface to pounce from, they use their strong back legs to propel themselves forward, stretching out their front legs so that they can grab the prey with their paws.

If they feel that the prey needs wrestling into submission, they will then roll onto their back so that they can hold it with their front paws and kick it with their back paws, attempting to rip the unsuspecting victim to shreds.

Playing with your cat will exercise its natural hunting instincts

HIGH JUMPERS

Cats are able to jump an incredible six times their own height, even without a run-up. This impressive skill proves very useful when hunting, as they can leap up onto tall trees or fences for a better vantage point, or even snatch their prey out of the air. It also comes in handy for escaping tricky situations, as they can make a speedy vertical getaway to places others can't reach.

The reason cats are much better at this than most other animals is due to their incredibly powerful back leg muscles and low body weight. Preparation is also key; before a jump, a cat will crouch down like a coiled spring, ensuring the maximum amount of force for liftoff. To land on their chosen perch, they then pull themselves up with their back legs and grip with their front claws. This is why you need to be very careful with their claws and only trim them if they get too long.

WHY DO CATS ALWAYS LAND ON THEIR FEET?

When falling from a great height, cats are usually able to turn themselves around in mid-air to land safely on their paws. Usually an animal would need something to push against in order to perform this rather difficult manoeuvre, but cats can do it without any help.

A cat's spine is flexible enough to be able to twist in opposite directions at the same time, which means that it can essentially spin in mid-air. By twisting the front half of its spine clockwise, and the back half anti-clockwise, it can push against itself to turn the right way up.

What's more, it can also make the front half of its body spin faster by pulling its front legs close into its body, just like an ice skater pulls in their arms to help them spin faster on the ice.

01 DO THE TWIST
As the cat starts to fall, it twists the front and back halves of its body in different directions.

02 IN A SPIN
By twisting in both directions, the cat pushes against itself to turn the right way up.

03 PAWS IN
By pulling its front legs in to its body, the cat causes its front half to twist faster than the back half.

04 SLOW IT DOWN
The cat flattens its body to act like a parachute, creating more air resistance to slow down its descent.

05 TOUCHDOWN
With all four paws facing downwards to absorb the impact, the cat can make a safe landing.

FAST FELINES

In the wild, cats have to always be on the lookout for potential predators and prey, and our pet cats have maintained this natural instinct. Even when they are snoozing, they use their super-sensitive ears, nose and whiskers to sense the world around them, and can spring into action at a moment's notice.

Just like their bigger relative, the cheetah, our kitties are quick sprinters, and can go from 0 to 48 kilometres (30 miles) per hour in a matter of seconds. They're able to reach these speeds by extending their powerful back legs in front of their front legs to gain momentum, and running on their toes so that a smaller portion of their feet touches the ground, creating less friction. In full sprint, they can also extend and flex their spine, stretching their body so that one stride is equal to three times their body length, enabling them to cover more ground.

SUPREME STABILITY

A cat's ability to walk along a narrow fence or shelf is mainly down to its tail. The tail is in fact an extension of the spine, and acts as a counterweight when they are trying to maintain their balance. If they feel themselves falling in one direction, they simply swing their tail in the opposite direction to realign their hips and shift their weight to keep them upright.

To help them tell which way up they are, or which direction they're falling in, cats use their inner ear as a compass. This is why a cat with an ear infection, or indeed no tail, may be a little unsteady on its paws.

Cats can traverse incredibly narrow ledges by using their tail to ensure perfect balance

When you have a cat, it is important not to be too emotionally invested in fragile knick-knacks

MISBEHAVIOUR EXPLAINER

Your cat's bad behaviour doesn't (always) come from their innate lust for chaos – it could be a sign that something is troubling them

We find our feline friends irresistible when they rub their head against us, snuggle with us, or adorably chase a feather toy around the room. The amount of cute cat photos and videos on the internet will attest to that! However, not all cat behaviour is so charming. You may have a cat that will not let you get a peaceful night's sleep, or a cat that tears your furniture to pieces. Luckily there is no malice behind any of these behaviours, and a lot of problems do have solutions. If your cat is a bit of a troublemaker then read on to find out what these behaviours mean and how you can discourage their naughty tendencies.

"THERE IS NO MALICE BEHIND ANY OF THESE BEHAVIOURS AND A LOT OF PROBLEMS DO HAVE SOLUTIONS"

First-time cat owners may be surprised by how loud even a little kitten can be

EXCESSIVE MEOWING

What it could mean if your cat is worryingly vocal

Meowing is your cat's best way to get your attention and is normal cat behaviour – though some cat breeds are naturally inclined to be more 'talkative' than others. The level of meowing that could be classed as excessive is personal to every cat. Your cat's meows are mostly likely to function as a greeting, a request for food or attention, or to be let in or out of the house. Yowls – long, drawn-out meows – are generally related to mating. If your cat is non-stop meowing they may be lonely or bored and need more stimulation and interaction. Your cat could have anxiety issues stemming from a change to their home or routine, and if they are elderly could be disoriented due to dementia. If you're unable to work out what your cat needs, then take them to a veterinarian to rule out any medical issues.

No item is safe on a shelf or table when you have a cat in your home

KNOCKING THINGS OVER

Try not to get too emotionally attached to anything that is fragile

Pushing various items off shelves, cabinets and tables is classic bad behaviour from cats. It's fun to watch when it isn't your knick-knacks being smashed to bits – but why do cats love doing this? According to science, it's not your cat being petty. Thanks to their innate hunting instincts, cats have an urge to test items to see if they are prey or might contain prey. Cats are quite intelligent, so it doesn't take long to work out that a candlestick is not a mouse, but a side effect to knocking things over is human attention. If you come running every time you hear something fall to the ground then your cat will use this to their advantage.

Your cat now decides what time you need to wake up — whether you like it or not!

RISING EARLY
Are you frequently woken up by the tickle of whiskers?

Has it been a long time since you've been able to sleep peacefully through the night without a furry paw batting you in the face? This may be down to differences in nature. Humans are diurnal (active in the day and resting at night), while cats are crepuscular — meaning they are most active at dawn and dusk. It just so happens that your kitty is feeling well-rested and playful at a time when you're still asleep. However, if your cat wakes you up begging and crying for food or attention, you can retrain them to stop this behaviour. If they're hungry, try using an automatic feeder in the morning and if they're bored, make sure they have enough play before bed time and some treat puzzles left out overnight.

BADLY BEHAVED FELINES

Fortunately, a lot of bad behaviour is just the expression of a problem that does have a solution

STEALING FOOD
Human food is dangerous for cats, so if your feline is stealing from your plate then it's time to set some boundaries. Always keep your food out of reach and don't give in to their begging.

BRINGING IN PREY
If your cat is too successful a hunter and brings home its prey, there are a number of ways you can discourage this. Fit your cat with a collar with a bell and make sure that a lot of your play with them simulates hunting.

CHEWING ON THINGS
If your cat is chewing your things to shreds you should take them to a vet, as it could be a sign of stomach problems or gum disease. It can also be an outlet for a cat who is anxious, stressed, or bored.

BITING
Cats can be easily overstimulated by touch, so a bite is a message that playtime is over. If your cat bites without provocation then it may be that you haven't noticed the warning signs in their body language, such as flat ears.

BULLYING
If one cat is fighting another, then you need to step in. Hissing and growling is a sign that the behaviour is getting too intense and it might be time to give both cats some space from each other.

Images © Getty Images

GOING OUTSIDE THE LITTER BOX

What to do if your cat refuses to use the litter box

If you've taken your cat to the vet to rule out any medical issues but they continue to pee and poop outside the litter box, you still have some more avenues to explore. It may be that your cat doesn't like the site of the box or the type of litter. Try out different litter types (unscented is usually best) and add another box to a different location in your home. Also try out boxes with or without a cover – some cats like privacy, others like a view when they're at their most vulnerable. Some cats will refuse the box if there is some mess in the litter, so always make sure to keep it as clean as you can to encourage them to use it.

Making a mess outside the litter box is one of the most common problems faced by cat owners around the world

Ruining a piece of expensive furniture is all in a day's work for a cat

SCRATCHING FURNITURE

Are your curtains in tatters thanks to your cat?

Just because you live with a cat doesn't mean you have to live with destroyed furniture. Scratching is normal, instinctive behaviour for cats – it keeps their claws sharp, marks territory in their home and generally gives your cat a bit of exercise. So your cat shouldn't be disciplined or punished for scratching furniture – they are probably only doing it because there is nothing else for them to scratch. You therefore always need to make sure you provide multiple purpose-made scratching posts in your home, and rub a bit of catnip against them to tempt your cat to try them out.

CAT MYTHS

Thought you knew everything there was to know about cats? Think again! Here are a few of the most common cat myths debunked...

WORDS NATALIE DENTON

Cats. So easy, so straightforward, you feel like you know what they want before they know what they want. One of the reasons for this is because cats have been pets for hundreds, if not thousands, of years, so it's hard not to feel like a bit of an expert, even if you don't own one yourself. But that's where most people are wrong, because a great many of the things we once took to be fact about our feline companions have now been proven to be false. Whether through scientific study and research, or just good old common sense, we now know a lot more about cats than ever before. Here are some of the most common cat myths, and why they are wrong.

"WE NOW KNOW A LOT MORE ABOUT CATS THAN EVER BEFORE"

Once we understand where we are going wrong with cats, we can start to get things right

CATS AREN'T LOVING

Just because they aren't needy, doesn't mean they don't love you

We all show love in different ways; that's what 'love language' is all about, and while dogs will perform somersaults at the mere sight of you, cats like to play things a bit more cool. But they do love you. A research project carried out by Oregon State University proved it. Signs that your cat loves you include: gently rubbing its head against you (bunting); purring at your touch; licking, grooming or kneading you; rolling on its back in your presence and exposing its belly; bringing you gifts of everything it can 'hunt' from toy mice to once live ones; sleeping on you; and approaching you with an upright but slightly curved tail. If you spot your cat doing any of these, it's trying to tell you those three little words...

Cats prefer twilight to no light, making the myth that they are nocturnal false. Dusk and dawn are actually their favourite parts of the day

CATS ARE NOCTURNAL
Cats may not keep the same hours as us, but they aren't night owls

Despite the vast majority of people presuming felines are nocturnal, they are in fact 'crepuscular', which means to be active or appearing at twilight. So they actually aren't out 'living it up' all hours of the night, but instead just around the hours of dusk and dawn. This is the reason your cat likes to rest, or take several cat naps during the day. They are recharging their batteries in order to have optimum energy during what they consider to be the prime stalking and hunting hours, a habit passed down from their much bigger, incredibly successful hunter ancestors. Cats' eyes are perfectly designed for low light, which gives them the upper hand during twilight, making it easier for them to sneak up and capture their prey be it a bird, mouse or even a frog, ready to deliver as a gift at your feet as you arise ready to start your day.

CATS LOVE CATNIP
While some cats love a bit of catnip, others just say no

Catnip, a perennial herb from the mint family, sends most cats loopy – one sniff of the stuff and they're rolling, rubbing, flipping and flopping themselves all over the place until they eventually zone out in a drugged-like state. This happens because when the cat inhales the nepetalactone from the plant (whether dried, cut, oil or live), it bonds to the receptors inside their nose, which stimulates the sensory neurons that link to the brain. But while it's long been believed that all cats love a little sniff of catnip, recent evidence suggests otherwise, with experts now estimating that in fact only 50-75% of cats are affected by the plant. Apparently the young and old are less likely to react to the effects of catnip, while it has also been suggested that some cats may lack a certain gene that makes them able to react to it, as the catnip response is actually something that is inherited.

Some cats go gaga for catnip while others, around 25-50% aren't bothered by the stuff in the slightest

YOU CAN'T TRAIN A CAT

With time, treats and a whole lot of patience, anything is possible – even training

Yes, dogs are agreed to be the more 'obedient' or 'trainable' domesticated animal, but that's not to say cats can't be taught a trick or two, far from it in fact. As cats are very intelligent animals some animal trainers would even go so far as to say they are easier to teach. The key to training your cat is to understand its natural instincts and remember that they respond to positive reinforcement (ie treats – the more fragrant and 'favourite' the better and eventually a clicker), rather than punishments. To begin with, show your cat something simple. As soon as it mimics or repeats the gesture, reward the cat with a treat. Practise this several times, but stop before it bores them.

"Stay", "come" and "down" are just a few of the basic commands a cat can do. Once mastered, they'll be ready for something a touch more creative.

Whoever said "cats are easier than dogs", didn't own a cat; they're harder than they look

CATS ARE LOW MAINTENANCE

Cats can be as cool as dogs, but they are not without their demands

So yes, compared to a dog – which needs walking, its poop scooped, training, and a lot of fuss and attention – cats are a low maintenance pet, but that's not to say owning one is a walk in the park. First of all, like dogs, they shed a lot, so vacuuming is a daily chore, as is changing the litter box. When it comes to personality, they are definitely one of the most strong-willed of creatures and getting on their bad side can result in a nasty scratch or nip, not to mention the annoying social hours they keep (twilight) and their penchant for dead animal gift giving. And don't forget with those great claws, comes great damage, as many a sofa or curtain can testify.

CATS HATE WATER

Avoid giving your kitty a bath

To say "all cats hate water" is simply untrue. Just as all humans are different, so too are our feline friends and some of them actually have a penchant for a little paddle. Take for example the Bengal cat or the Turkish Van. These are two breeds who love a dip. The Bengal cat came into being after being bred from the Asian Leopard, a renowned strong swimmer amongst the big cat community, while the Turkish Van hails from Turkey's Lake Van region. Its love of water long ago earned it the nickname 'the swimming cat'. What's more, thanks to its naturally water-repellent cashmere-esque fur, the latter doesn't even need towelling off after a swim.

Granted, most cats hate water, but others actually like a little dip, take the Bengal or Turkish Van, for example

MORE MYTHS DEBUNKED

Cats are too complicated to be pigeonholed. Here are some other ways they might surprise you...

CATS HATE DOGS

Certain breeds of cats and dogs are known for getting along better than others, and the age they are introduced can have an impact. Ideally give each their own area of the home, keep their toys separate, and show equal amounts of love.

CATS ALWAYS LAND ON THEIR FEET

Although cats have an inbuilt balancing system known as the 'righting reflex', enabling them to right themselves during a fall to land on their paws, if they fell from a great height they could break bones, and from too low they could hit the ground on their side.

CATS NEED FRIENDS

Most cats prefer to be the only cat in their kingdom, and won't take kindly to you introducing a new cat to the home, or as they'll see it, an intruder. The exception to this is if you have cats that grow up together.

Milk and cream can actually make your cat sick, so give them water, preferably from a running source, instead

CATS LOVE DRINKING MILK

Just like the prickly hedgehog, don't give cats milk

It's such a classic association – cats and milk – but in actuality cats are lactose intolerant and definitely shouldn't be given milk to drink. Lacking the all-important lactase enzyme in their intestines means they can't digest the sugar lactose that features in milk, resulting in vomiting, diarrhoea, and stomach cramps – and the same is true of substitute milk products such as soy or almond milk. Instead, kittens should drink their mother's milk, or a specifically designed replacement such as kitten milk formula, for the first few months before being weaned on to solids at around ten weeks. Instead of milk, give your cat wet food and water. Research suggests they prefer water from a running source rather than a still saucer, such as from a fountain style dispenser.

CATS ARE DANGEROUS TO PREGNANT WOMEN

Toxoplasmosis is only found in cats who go outdoors to hunt and eat rodents – if this sounds like your pet then it's wise to ask someone else to change its litter box. However, if your cat stays indoors all the time, then your risk is said to be very low.

DECLAWING IS HARMLESS

Declawing is painful to the cat, and what's more it can cause infection, lameness and in the same way high-heel shoes are bad for human backs, declawing changes the way a cat's foot meets the ground and causes spinal problems.

CATS CAN SEE BETTER IN THE DARK

Cats are thought to see six to eight times better than we can in the dark, but their real strength is in low-light rather than in pitch black, such as during the hours of twilight when their hunting gene comes out to play.

Images © Getty Images, Alamy

HOW TO TRAIN YOUR CAT

Cats might not be as easy to teach as their canine counterparts, but there are plenty of tricks that they can master

WORDS LAURA MEARS

The best way to train cats is with positive reinforcement; psychologists call it operant conditioning. The aim is to link cues with behaviours, and behaviours with treats. To get started, choose a food your cat really likes, and invest in a training tool called a clicker.

A clicker makes a sound when you press it. Your first task is to teach your cat to associate that sound with the treat.

Find a place with no distractions and spend five or ten minutes working with your cat using the clicker. Short, frequent training sessions are best. To begin with, just click and reward on repeat until your cat starts to anticipate the arrival of a treat whenever they hear the sound. Once they've mastered that, you're ready to start teaching tricks.

For each one, choose a simple word or action such as "sit" or "lie down" as your cue, and use your clicker to tell your cat when they've got it right. Mark the exact moment they perform the trick, and always follow up with a treat.

7 COMMANDS TO TEACH YOUR CAT

1 SIT
A classic dog trick, sit is a surprisingly easy command for many cats. Start by luring them into position with a treat. Hold it just in front of their nose and gently lift upwards so they're looking at your hand. Then move slowly forward. As your cat follows, they will naturally move into a sit. Click and reward.

> "FIND A PLACE WITH NO DISTRACTIONS AND SPEND FIVE MINUTES WORKING WITH YOUR CAT"

2 RECALL
Recall can be a lifesaver, especially for outdoor cats. One of the best times to teach it is at dinner. Call out your cat's name, or a special word like "come", every time you set their food down. That way, they'll quickly learn to associate the cue with a very big treat. Then you can start practising in different situations. Start by calling them just a short distance and offering a favourite food as a reward. Build up slowly, moving further away, and then just out of sight. As they improve, you can try calling them from different parts of the house. And finally, you can graduate to the garden.

3 LIE DOWN
Some cats will lie down on any small object: a piece of paper, a box, a blanket, even a square of masking tape. You can train them to do this on command by 'capturing' the behaviour. As soon as you see them settle, click and reward. If your cat needs a bit more help to find the right position, try luring them with a treat. Hold it just in front of their nose and lower slowly towards the ground. Now pull back a little. They should follow, bowing down and stretching out.

With a bit of patience, and lots of treats, you can train your cat to perform these seven simple tricks on command

4 TARGET

This trick is a great way to distract your cat. Find a wooden spoon and rub something tasty and smelly on the end. Tuna works well. Now hold it out for your cat to investigate. As soon as they touch it with their nose, say "target", click, and reward.

5 GENTLE

Cats can flip from soft and sweet to claws and teeth in the blink of an eye. Training them to be gentle is all about redirection. The first step is to make aggression as boring for them as possible. Cats love movement, so fight the urge to pull away. Instead go completely still and say the word "gentle". When they stop, click and reward. Now withdraw your hand. You can either walk away, teaching them that hurting you stops the game completely, or you can offer them something much more exciting, like a fast-moving wand toy.

6 FIST BUMP

Cats are very dextrous; they naturally use their paws to fish for food. This makes tricks like "fist bump", "high five", and "shake" accessible even to beginners. Start out by popping a treat inside a paper cup. Put it down, and let your cat investigate. When they reach out with their paw to knock the cup over, give them a click. Now, try holding the cup. Click as soon as they touch it. Then, try covering the top of the cup with your fingers so that they have to touch your hand. Finally, you can remove the cup altogether.

7 HIGH FIVE

This trick is an extension of the fist bump. Once your cat has mastered the art of tapping your closed hand, you can teach them to touch your open palm. Start out by offering your hand face up. Click as soon as their paw touches your skin. Once that is sorted, try holding your hand out with your palm facing forward.

A clicker marks the exact moment your cat performed the trick

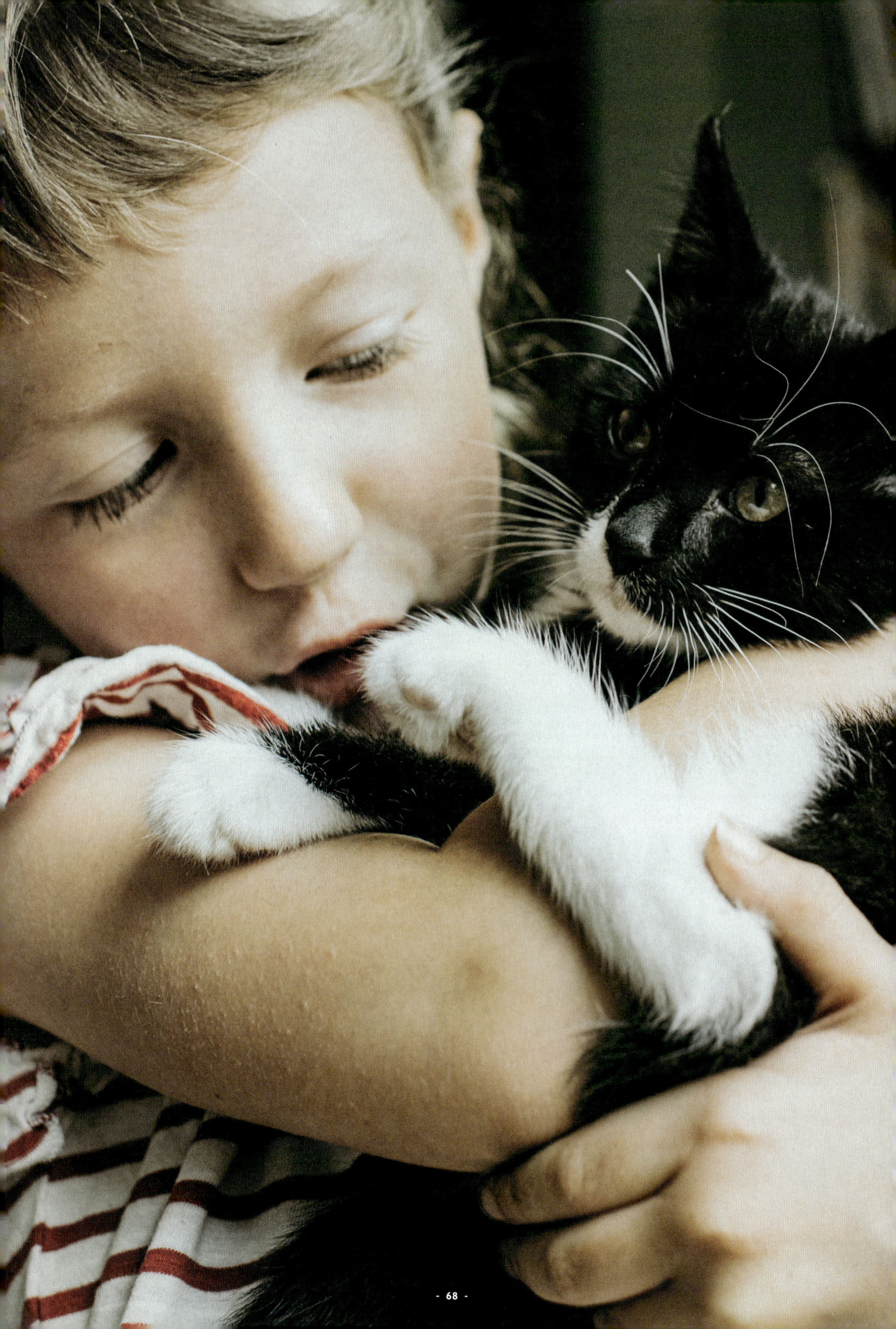

CATS AND CHILDREN

Here are a few key things to consider to ensure cats and kids grow up as the best of friends

WORDS ELLA CARTER

There are so many benefits that our pet cats can provide – but one of most rewarding is how much of a positive effect the family kitty can have on kids. As well as being an ever-present, fluffy friend to play with, keeping pets can teach kids about empathy, kindness and responsibility, which in turn can help to boost self-esteem. Kids can develop close bonds with their pets and find it easier to express themselves when spending time with them. Growing up with a cat (or other pets) can also mean less allergies in adult life.

Before you introduce your family to their new best friend, it's important to take steps to understand the needs of your individual cats and children and how they interact. Here are a few key things to consider to ensure that your new cat becomes a much-loved and well-cared-for member of your family.

HOW TO ACHIEVE A PEACEFUL CAT AND CHILD RELATIONSHIP

1 RIGHT PERSONALITY

If you have young kids and toddlers, advice from Battersea and Cats Protection is that kittens aren't necessarily the best fit. They need some training and have lots of energy for play fighting with sharp claws, which is easier for bigger kids to understand and manage but hard for little ones to stay scratch-free. Instead, adopting an adult cat can be a great option.

Temperament is really important when rehoming a cat, as just like us, cats have their own personal preference. It's important for your cat's wellbeing and a harmonious family life that your new fluffy friend fits in well. The adoption centre will help you to find a cat that is relaxed in their environment and not spooked or phased by changes or noises around them (a household with kids is a noisy one!). Other cat qualities to look for are a confident and friendly nature and enjoying physical contact and cuddles.

2 KEEP A CLOSE EYE

It goes without saying that even if cats and children are firm friends, they should always be supervised when they're spending time together. This is especially important if you've only just introduced children to a new cat, as they'll still be getting to know each other. Kids will need your guidance on how to act with a new cat, and cats will need someone to diffuse a situation if they feel anxious or scared and things get too much. Supervising these interactions is essential to ensure good first impressions are made, and avoid any scratches or bites.

Never force an interaction with your cat, and be sure that kids understand that they shouldn't do this too! Children will mimic adult behaviour and so it's important to set a good example, to ensure that your new cat feels safe and secure with kids around.

Cuddles and purrs can reduce stress and have a calming effect, especially for children who suffer from anxiety

3 SAFE ENVIRONMENT

It's important to give your cat some child-free space in your home, so that if things get too much, they can slink away for a bit of quiet time to rest and recharge. Cats are solitary by nature, and so some quiet time will always be needed – especially if your home is busy and noisy!

Ensure that children understand that even though their cat loves them, they shouldn't be disturbed when they're sleeping or resting on their own. You could make use of baby gates to separate areas for cats to retreat to, or invest in some cat-friendly accessories such as a cat tree to enable your kitty to perch up high, out of harm's way.

It's a good idea to put your cat's essentials such as food and water bowls in these cat-only spaces too, as being disturbed, frightened or annoyed while eating or drinking will be quite irritating for a hungry cat!

"CATS ARE SOLITARY BY NATURE AND SO SOME QUIET TIME WILL ALWAYS BE NEEDED"

SAFE INTRODUCTIONS

Here are some key steps to take when it's time to introduce your family to its newest member

GIVE SOME SPACE
Don't let kids crowd a cat – and be ready to diffuse a situation calmly if your cat shows signs of being anxious or scared.

NO TOUCHING
Let cats feel comfortable before kids can cuddle! Encourage little ones to let the cat come to them first and not to grab or force affection.

CALM VIBES
When your cat comes home, encourage kids to sit still and be calm and patient while your cat explores its new surroundings.

BE PATIENT
It could take minutes for kids and cats to become best friends, or you might need to repeat these steps over and over – either way, it's worth it!

FIRST IMPRESSIONS ARE IMPORTANT
Before your new cat arrives, prepare your kids by talking to them about the responsibilities and requirements of having a pet.

KEEP TREATS HANDY
Have some delicious treats close by and let your kids reward your cat when they come close. This establishes an association between your kids and receiving tasty snacks.

4 UNDERSTAND THE CAT

Cats are very physically expressive, and so it's a really good idea to teach kids to watch how their kitty is behaving to interpret how they're feeling, so they can respect the cat's needs. For example, a tail swishing from side to side is the sign of an angry cat, but a tail curving down with a little lift at the tip means your cat is peaceful and relaxed.

It's also important to ensure kids understand a cat's boundaries – for example a soft, gentle stroke on the head or under the chin is usually much appreciated, whereas attempting to tickle the tummy will in many cases result in a swift nip.

5 SPEND QUALITY TIME

Encouraging kids to spend time with their cats is the best way to initiate bonding. Your cat will come to realise that kids are fun and nice to be around, which will be wonderful for children to experience. While you're still getting to know each other, encourage games that don't involve touching – for example playing with cat toys or using delicious treats to do a bit of training (it can be done!). This will mean that your cat grows in confidence and feels safe and secure having fun with kids, and vice versa. This is really important for building up trust between little ones and their furry pals.

6 TAKE BABY STEPS

If your cat is used to having your full attention, the arrival of a new baby can completely obliterate their world, and so it's important you take some steps to make sure that things go smoothly. When it comes to first introducing them, do so in a neutral space and let your cat approach at their own pace. They might be really keen to sniff and get acquainted with the new human, or they might appear disinterested. Don't force them and let them take their time – but always be sure to supervise any interaction.

You can also lay the groundwork before the baby is born. Let your cat explore new baby items and you could even try playing noises of babies quietly to get cats used to the sounds.

Quality time with their cat will allow your child to form an amazing bond

Keep an eye on your cat to see how they're faring with being introduced to new arrivals

DOES YOUR CAT HAVE FEELINGS?

There's more to a cat than just their natural instincts – they also experience a range of emotions and figuring out how they feel is key to boosting the pet-owner bond

WORDS BECKY BRADBURY

Cats are notorious for doing what pleases them. But they shouldn't be cast off as uncaring, selfish creatures, especially as there is an ever-growing body of research proving what cat owners have always intuited – that our feline friends do have feelings.

A common mistake is to expect a cat to act like us. Human beings have evolved to communicate emotions through their facial expressions, while domestic cats have descended from solitary wild animals. As independent hunters, their survival has not depended upon being part of a pack. With this in mind, it's no wonder the two species have very different ways of expressing how they feel.

It's also unfair to compare cats to dogs. Cats have simply not undergone the same extent of socialising and training as our canine friends. Plus, with their wagging tails and slobbery licks, it's obvious when a dog is in a good mood, whereas a cat's behaviour is far more subtle.

One animal behaviourist championing cats as sensitive beings is Dr John Bradshaw. In his book, *Cat Sense*, he writes: "Cats live in the present, neither reflecting on the past nor planning for the future." This reasoning suggests that emotions motivate much of a cat's behaviour.

However, there is always a danger of anthropomorphizing our pets. Although cats do have some emotions in common with us, they don't share the full remit.

FEAR

Studies suggest babies are born with feelings, one of which is fear. A kitten also experiences terror and, throughout a cat's life, many of its automatic reactions will be based on fear.

When a cat is afraid it will flee, freeze or fight. The latter is expressed through aggressive actions, such as hissing, spitting or growling, and the evolutionary reason behind this response is to drive away whatever is threatening it. Cats also experience the involuntary piloerection reflex, where the fur on their back and tail stands on end in an attempt to look bigger and more threatening.

This hostile behaviour could also be a sign of annoyance or anger. But whatever the emotion, it's important to back away at this point before the cat lashes out, either by scratching, swotting or biting.

> "MANY OF A CAT'S AUTOMATIC REACTIONS WILL BE BASED ON FEAR"

Cats feel fear from when they are kittens and a lot of their instinctual behaviour is fear based

74

SIGNS OF ANXIETY

When a cat acts up it's not being naughty. Chances are it's anxious, so watch out for the following behaviour:

- Hiding or running away
- Aggressive and destructive behaviour
- Excessive meowing
- Non-stop grooming
- Litter box avoidance
- Restlessness

ANXIETY

Just like humans and dogs, cats also suffer from anxiety. Continuously adopting the fear-based behaviours described is a sign of an anxious cat, but there are other signals, too. These include the destruction of objects, excessive meowing, non-stop grooming, a change in eating habits and continuous pacing. Plus, if your cat won't let you out of its sight, it's possible they have separation anxiety.

There are many reasons why a cat could be anxious. A big change might be the cause. For example, moving to a new house, the adoption of a new pet, or a new person (or baby) moving in. If your pet is displaying signs of anxiety, try to keep things consistent for them and ensure they have a quiet place to hide and rest, such as a room of their own or a cat tower.

"A CAT'S LOW MOOD IS OFTEN CAUSED BY CHANGE"

HAPPINESS

A cat is happy when all of its needs are being met. While the hiss of an angry cat leaves little doubt about how its feeling, a joyful cat's body language and behaviour are not so clear.

Expressive eyes, a relaxed posture, ears facing forwards, and an upright tail with a little curve at its tip are all signs of a content cat. Sounds to listen out for include purring, chirruping and high-pitched meows, and if your cat washes itself, sleeps or plays in your presence, it feels at ease alongside you.

A cat who shows you physical affection is usually in a good mood, too.

SADNESS

Life has its highs and lows and, just like us, cats can experience feelings of sadness. While we can never know for sure what's going on inside a cat's mind, the behaviours they exhibit when feeling down are similar to the symptoms of depression in human beings. These include eating less, sleeping more and a loss of interest in formerly enjoyable activities.

A cat's low mood is often caused by a change in routine, but it might be down to illness, so if you can't determine an obvious cause, see your vet. Another possibility is that a cat is grieving a loved one, whether it's a human companion or a fellow pet they are missing. Again, this is proof that a cat's emotional range is regularly underestimated.

SIGNS OF DEPRESSION

Big changes can make your cat feel down, so if you switch up your routine be wary of the following:

- Low-pitched, mournful yowls
- Loss of appetite or over-eating
- Poor grooming habits
- Sleeping more
- Running away and hiding
- Loss of interest in things they once enjoyed

SIGNS OF LOVE

Cats have stronger emotions than they're often given credit for. Here's how they show their affection:

- Greeting you at the door
- Gentle head-butts or 'bunting'
- Showing their tummy to you
- Licking, grooming or kneading you
- Slow, long blinks at you
- Hanging out in your space

LOVE

Cats might be independent creatures by nature, but animal behaviourists believe felines are, in most cases, very fond of their owners. A cat's temperament, however, will affect how these positive emotions are shown. For example, for one cat simply being in the same room as somebody could be a sign of its love, while another will sit on its object of affection's lap and demand to be petted.

Researchers have also recently discovered that, just like children and dogs, cats form emotional attachments to their caregivers. So, the presence of a caregiver can make a cat feel secure, safe and comfortable. But as cats are, at heart, solitary animals, they probably don't have an innate need to form a strong, secure attachment with their owners. The bond is more likely down to factors like personality, early socialisation and how they are kept.

EMPATHY

It has long been believed that cats are incapable of showing empathy. However, a 2020 study on emotion recognition in cats demonstrated that felines integrate visual and auditory cues to recognise human emotions, specifically anger and happiness. The experiment also proved that cats adapt and modulate their behaviour according to how they perceive human emotion.

Although the research didn't prove that a cat would comfort an upset human being, many owners can recall times when their cat gave them affection while they were feeling down. Even though it's not possible to prove a cat can understand what we're going through, we can be sure they are in possession of social skills crucial to strengthening the cat-owner bond.

GUILT AND JEALOUSY

Humans have the ability to self-reflect and, as such, are able to develop a concept of self and an understanding of human values. Cats, however, do not have the same capabilities. Therefore, they are unable to feel our more complex emotions, such as guilt and shame.

When a cat gets told off for scratching the sofa or jumping up onto the kitchen worktop, it might run away with its tail between its legs. This might seem like a guilty response, but its body language is actually conveying fear at the scolding it just received.

Likewise, envy is veering into human emotional territory. Although a cat may display behaviour that looks like jealousy, such as pushing a fellow feline out of the way to get to the food bowl first, it's actually their territorial instinct kicking in when they feel the need to compete for scarce resources.

SIGNS OF HAPPINESS

When a cat is content, it's not always obvious. Here are the tell-tale signs:

- Playful behaviour
- Social sleeping
- A relaxed posture
- Healthy appearance
- A good appetite
- Purring and high-pitched meows

5 REASONS YOUR CAT FOLLOWS YOU AROUND

Eat, love, play. There are several different reasons why your precious pet follows (usually very closely) in your footsteps...

WORDS NATALIE DENTON

1 THEY'RE BORED

You are your cat's sun, moon and stars – you're literally the centre of their universe. You control everything from when and what they eat to providing them with love, shelter and even entertainment. While they are well adept at amusing themselves, they see you as a 'play thing' and provider of fun (amongst other things), so don't be surprised if they follow you around like a puppy until you give them exactly what they need: attention. This is particularly the case with house cats, who don't have the same hunting opportunities as those who are allowed outdoors.

2 THEY'RE HUNGRY

Just like children, be they toddlers or teenagers, cats will bug you when hunger strikes, albeit in their case with an affectionate purr and gentle stroke of their tail against your legs. They'll know almost to the second when it's feeding time, not only because of their internal body clock but more so based on your routine, which they've spent time studying to the point where they can expertly preempt your every move, knowing exactly when to fall in step, ready to pounce on their grub as it appears, almost as if they were in the wild.

3 THEY'RE FEELING NEEDY

When cats feel most anxious, stressed or scared, you'll find that they are more inclined to 'cling' to your side in a bid to reinstate their usual sense of security and emotional wellbeing. Factors such as stormy weather, fireworks, parties, illness, change of home, the arrival of a new baby or pet, and separation anxiety – such as if you've been away for a while or on holiday – can all have an emotional and physical impact on your pet. As super-sensitive animals, even the slightest change to their world can upset them. For example, something as seemingly insignificant as changing your pet's usual brand of food can cause them to feel in need of some extra love and snuggles.

4 THEIR CURIOSITY IS AROUSED

In short, cats find humans, and human behaviour interesting. Whether it's following you into the bathroom and watching as you use the toilet, or tracing your every move as you move absent-mindedly around the kitchen to cook; cat's weren't labelled as 'curious' for nothing. What's more, scent is a big thing for our feline friends, so when you move to areas where there are stronger aromas – such as the bathroom or kitchen – your cute companion's curiosity is naturally aroused and therefore they're sure to be close behind.

5 IT'S A TERRITORY THING

Just like babies, domesticated cats quickly learn to depend on their human parents for survival, perhaps more than many people realise – dispelling the myth that cats are the 'independent pet' that can take care of themselves. In return your cat will show you it loves you. One of the ways it does this is by marking your (and therefore its) territory with its scent, just as it would in the wild. At home this means following you around, rubbing themselves on anything in yours and their proximity, and leaving behind their scent to let others know that this home has been claimed. From chair legs to your legs, your cat will be diligently bagsying everything and anything you own.

BECOME A CAT WHISPERER

Spending time cuddling and playing with your feline friend is always rewarding, but learning to communicate with your cat can take your relationship to a new level of purrfection

WORDS BEE GINGER

Many people assume dogs make the best companions, but that's because they have never taken the time to really explore and understand cats. Cats are a highly intelligent species that can understand up to as many as 50 words, including their name (although most cat owners admit to having many names for their feline friends). Scientists have learned through a series of studies that cats have developed their own unique communication system in the form of various vocalisations that they use to communicate their wants and needs. But the research into feline behaviours doesn't need to be restricted to a lab – by studying your furry friend you can learn how to better communicate with your moggy.

AN ANCIENT DIALECT

While we humans can struggle to understand our cats, they worked us out thousands of years ago

There's no doubt that humans are an extremely intelligent species, capable of incredible feats. And yet, despite our achievements to date, mastering fluent feline continues to evade us. Thankfully our furry friends have done the hard work for us, enabling two species to communicate effectively for millennia.

It probably didn't take the first domesticated cats long to realise that humans struggle to interpret and therefore respond appropriately to their non-verbal cues, but instead of slinking back off into the wild, these crafty creatures developed a way of vocalising their wants and needs in a manner that we can understand. Vocalising is not something that cats really use to communicate with other cats, as they tend to instead use a complex combination of body language, touch, facial expressions and scents, which makes their ability to convey their meaning to humans via a series of different noises all the more remarkable. And their verbal abilities don't end there; they can also understand the meaning of many of the words that you use.

From "water" to "bowl" and "bird" to "food", cats can learn (through a process of repetition) to associate certain short words with corresponding actions. For example, if you say "food" while heading towards the kitchen, your cat will soon know to follow you for a tasty snack.

"BY STUDYING YOUR FURRY FRIEND YOU CAN LEARN HOW TO BETTER COMMUNICATE"

MEOW IT'S TIME TO LISTEN

Knowing what your cat means can be tricky. Here are some different types of vocalisations to help you distinguish between a request and a protest

SHORT MEOW Standard greeting

MULTIPLE MEOWS Excited greeting

MID-PITCH MEOW Plea for something like food or water

DRAWN-OUT MRRROOOOW Requesting or demanding something

LOW-PITCH MRRROOOOOWWW Usually a complaint or signal of displeasure

LOWER THAN MID-PITCH MEEOOOOOOWWW A request for something such as food

HIGH-PITCH RRRROWW! An expression of anger, pain or fear

CHATTER (RAPID TEETH CHATTERING) Excitement, frustration

CHIRRUP (A CROSS BETWEEN A MEOW AND A PURR WITH RISING INFLECTION) Friendly greeting sound, often used by a mother cat to call to her kittens

PURR Invites close contact or attention

HISS A strong sign of distress, fear or discomfort

Every cat develops its own unique 'vocabulary' with which to speak to the humans in its family. Comprising a mix of purrs, meows and other sounds, a cat can deploy as many as 100 different noises. In comparison, dogs are limited to around ten

IT'S HOW YOU SAY IT

When it comes to communicating with your cat, how you speak is just as important as what you say

When talking to your cat, be sure your tone of voice matches the message you wish to convey. A slightly raised tone of voice indicates friendliness, whereas a lowered tone could indicate displeasure. A command tone is also important for your cat to learn so that they know when they have done something wrong. You could even make a short unexpected noise, like a hand clap, in order to emphasise a "no" command. Make sure to be consistent and not pet your cat when reprimanding them, as this will only confuse them.

MAKE TIME FOR YOUR MOGGY

Putting time aside to spend with your cat is hugely beneficial for both of you

Your cat is part of your family, but you can't take it for granted that your four-legged friend knows this. They have to be shown. The best way to do this is to include your cat in your daily activities wherever possible. One way to do this is when you are preparing a meal. While you're chopping and seasoning, talk to your cat as you go. By allowing your cat to see what you are doing and listen to the sound of your voice they will feel engaged with, which in turn will have the added benefit of helping them to interact with other people and animals with more confidence.

BLINKS, WINKS AND KISSES

Taking the time to understand how your cat expresses affection can bring you closer together

Do you often notice your cat blinking slowly at you? This is their way of saying "I love you". The next time your cat blinks at you try to reciprocate the gesture. Sit a short distance away from them then, while looking at your cat, slowly close your eyes. Wait a moment before opening them again and you will see your love blink being returned.

Another signal of affection that cats commonly use when greeting others of the same species is a 'nose kiss', by which they gently touch noses. You can share a similar experience with your furry friend by crouching down next to them (only when they are relaxed and feeling calm) and curling your index finger in towards the palm of your hand (the shape almost resembles a cat's nose). Now slowly extend your arm and allow your cat to come over and greet you in their own feline language.

CONFRONTING BAD BEHAVIOUR

Your cat may well be your best friend, but sometimes they will need to be gently reminded that they aren't in fact the boss

Playtime is crucial for kittens because it helps them to learn and develop vital skills that they will need later on in life, but as with youngsters of every kind, sometimes things can get a little rough. When a sibling is being too heavy-pawed, their playmate will squeak loudly to alert them, thereby encouraging the other kitten to tone things down. Yet while this is a useful signal between kittens, it's also a trick that you can borrow when it comes to disciplining your cat.

If your moggy gets a bit carried away while playing with you, try saying "ouch" consistently. In time your cat will learn to associate this short, sudden, higher-pitched sound with the need to be gentle while playing. Another option is to gently place your cat on the floor every time they bite or claw you. They will soon realise that getting too aggressive spells the end of playtime.

TWITCHING WITH CURIOSITY

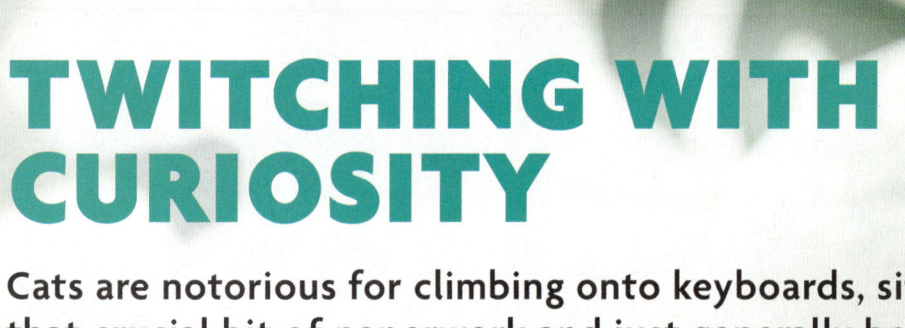

Cats are notorious for climbing onto keyboards, sitting on that crucial bit of paperwork and just generally being nosey – but their natural inquisitiveness should be cherished

Cats are naturally curious animals and are great fun to play and interact with. After all, it's no coincidence that the internet is awash with millions of videos of cats performing all sorts of wild antics. Each cat has its own individual character and set of needs, wants and likes, one of which is closely following their human companions to see what they are up to. If you find your cat leaning over something that you are doing, this is an indication that they too are interested and want to be involved – which is admittedly not always very practical, especially when it comes to trying to read a newspaper, a pursuit that often results in your cat nudging it out of your hands, shredding it to pieces or claiming it for themselves! However, when they aren't trying to distract you, cats have been known to examine their owner's actions intently and then mimic them.

YOU NEED TO UNDERSTAND HISS

To ensure that your cat is happy and stress-free it's vital that you can decipher what their behaviour really means

Your cat will use many different verbal and non-verbal signals to communicate with both humans and other animals, and sometimes it's easy to misinterpret what they might be trying to say.

To a human, a hiss can easily be construed as a sign of aggression, but in fact it is the opposite. When a cat hisses it is expressing that it is stressed, in discomfort, scared or feeling threatened. If your cat hisses at you it is asking you to back off and leave it alone, a request that you should immediately respect and act upon if you wish to avoid further upsetting your cat and possibly getting a scratch for your troubles.

Another sign that your cat is in no mood to play is a whipping tail. If your moggy starts flicking their tail up and then bringing it back down at speed you'd be wise to pay attention and give it some space.

However, not all tail-related movements are a sign of distress. A question mark-shaped tail is an invitation to play, and a bum in the face is, from your cat's point of view, a huge gesture of friendship and affection.

You may also find that your cat will occasionally sit and stare open-mouthed at you. While it might be tempting to think that they are gazing in awe at their wonderful human, they are in fact using an organ unique to felines that enables them to taste scents in the air, which can be mighty useful when sniffing out potential threats and possible prey.

Position yourself a foot or two away for your cat to get the best view of your face

HOW CATS SEE HUMANS

Does your cat know you from Adam? Find out whether your cat really is a fickle fellow or if they are capable of having favourites...

WORDS NATALIE DENTON

According to scientific research, a cat's vision is thought to be very similar to that of a human – albeit one who suffers with colour blindness because of their comparative lack of cones (the receptors that see colour). With only two types of cones (compared to our three types), it's thought cats see reds and oranges more as shades of grey, while blue and yellow hues pop just fine. The result of our misaligned colour palettes can therefore mean your cat's view of you is more muted than you might have initially thought, and ultimately if you're blonde, your hair probably makes more of an impact on your pet than fiery tresses of red. But it's not all bad news for our moggy mates, as what they lack in cones, they make up for in rods (the receptors that are sensitive to light), as they can see six to eight times better in low light than we do, and their 200-degree vision (compared to our 180 degrees) makes them superior at spotting things in their periphery.

In terms of eyesight, cats prefer things close but not too close, as they lack the muscles that would allow them to focus on objects right under their nose, which is where their whiskers come in. Similarly they can't discern things far away, as according to cats.org.uk, felines need to be no more than 20 feet (six metres) to see an object clearly, while humans are said to manage five times that distance. So if you want your pet to see you, really see you, then just make sure you stand a few metres back.

THE LOOK OF LOVE

A University of Oregon study published by the journal *Current Biology* discovered that cats view their owners as much more than just a source of food. The experiment, which repeatedly separated and then reunited cats with their owners for a few minutes at a time, discovered that the majority of the animals displayed a 'secure' attachment style – meaning the cats weren't distressed at being left alone, were curious about their new surroundings, and displayed a positive reaction when eventually reunited with their owner, debunking the myth that cats aren't as loving as more, seemingly, dependent pets. In addition to this, the research goes on to credit domesticated cats with emotional intelligence, the suggestion being that cats choose to (or sometimes not) love their owners.

BIG CAT MAMMAS

In an interview with *National Geographic*, cat behaviour expert and author of *Cat Sense*, John Bradshaw, stated that after decades of study and observation, he believes that cats actually see us as bigger versions of their own species, unlike dogs, who apparently see humans as different from themselves. The reason being that cats, unlike their canine counterparts, don't adapt their social behaviour when interacting with humans. For example, a cat will hold their tail up in the air; sit on top of, closely or next to their owner; rub themselves around and up against their caregiver's legs; and even go as far as to 'groom' them with a little lick or two. All of these actions are actually displays of social affection cats do if they are familiar with, fond of, or related to one another. John even goes further to explain that when a cat 'kneads' humans with a repetitive pawing action, it's evoking the same affectionate and communicative touch it would have used on its mother as a kitten, much like it does when it raises its tail and rubs against you. Ultimately what all this touchy-feely communication means is that, scientifically as well as heartwarmingly, your cat really does see you as family.

SMELL AND SOUND OVER SIGHT

When it comes to telling one human from another, most cats are not all that. In fact it's been suggested in a study by the University of Texas and Pennsylvania State University that while cats are very skilled at recognising and distinguishing the faces of their fellow felines, when it comes to us Homo sapiens, we all look the same. The experiment saw a series of cats shown one picture of their owner's face and another of a stranger. If they selected the picture of their handler they would receive a treat. The study concluded that the cats only correctly identified their owner half of the time. However, when the cats were asked to choose between a picture of a cat they 'knew' as opposed to one they didn't, they secured the treat over 90 percent of the time. Instead it's widely theorised that like other mammals, cats use their keener sense of smell and sound to know that you are you, with a 2013 study from Tokyo University confirming the latter. Using a collection of voice recordings, the researchers discovered that cats are more likely to twitch their ears when they hear their human's voice, and completely ignore that of a stranger's.

It's widely assumed, therefore, that rather than recognising you on sight alone, your cat is far more likely to react and respond to you based on things such as the sound of your voice, the natural scent carried on your skin and hair, and even learn from your habits, such as the way you move, walk, sit, stroke them and even things like the way you open a cupboard or a door.

So in summary your cat can see you, albeit slightly blurry depending on how far away you are, perhaps not in the right colour scheme, and as a bigger version of themselves, but they see you. What's more, your cat does know you, perhaps not by your face, but it is able to tell your voice, movement and scent apart from those of a stranger, and even from the various other people sharing or regularly visiting your home. Finally, the affectionate signals your moggy sends you are its way of letting you know it not only sees and knows you, but it loves you too.

> *"CATS ARE MORE LIKELY TO TWITCH THEIR EARS WHEN THEY HEAR THEIR HUMAN'S VOICE"*

Your cat will be touchy feely if they see you as family

A CAT'S VISION
The colours that our friends can detect

Due to a comparative lack of cones – the receptors in the eye that distinguish colour – it's widely thought that cats are a tad colour blind, commonly confusing red and orange shades. Blue and yellow tones, however, are the colours felines can recognise best, so the next time you shop for a new toy for your favourite moggy, perhaps go for one in a hue that will have the most impact.

Cats see blue and yellow shades the best, but reds are much harder for them to distinguish

Your cat certainly sees you, although you may be slightly blurry

SIGNS YOUR CAT MAY BE ILL

Beyond obvious indicators, such as bleeding, swelling or limping, keep an eye out for any of these warning signs – your cat might need your help

WORDS JO COLE

1 APPEARANCE OR BEHAVIOUR

Always pay attention to your cat's behaviour and appearance because any changes might be a sign that something is wrong. Is your cat suddenly sitting hunched over, or tilting their head? Maybe they aren't grooming as much and their fur is matted or dull, or it might be they are grooming more than usual. Are they sleeping more or less than normal, or have more or less energy? Is your typically friendly feline now lashing out, or hiding themselves away? Have they stopped jumping on objects, or lost interest in playing? There might be an obvious reason why a change happens, but check with a vet just in case.

2 APPETITE AND WEIGHT

If your cat is a fickle eater, noticing a change in appetite can be tricky. However, monitor this as best you can because increased/decreased appetite or thirst can be a sign something is amiss. Dental issues can make a cat picky with their food; a hungry cat who is also thirsty may have a metabolic disease; and a cat with no appetite but increased thirst might have liver or kidney problems. Drastic weight loss obviously means a trip to the vets, but gradual weight loss can be a sign of chronic illness. Get used to running your hands along your cat's back and ribs. If they start to feel bonier, talk to your vet.

3 TOILET TROUBLE

Being a litter tray detective is a good way to find clues of any health problems. One of the most obvious indicators – diarrhoea – might be a sign of parasites or other intestinal problems. If left untreated, not only will the initial cause get worse, but your cat could become dehydrated. At the other end of the spectrum, small, hard stools might be a sign of kidney disease. Increased urine could signal problems with holding water,

> *"IT ISN'T UNUSUAL FOR CATS TO VOMIT FROM TIME TO TIME"*

while less urine could be kidney or bladder problems. This also explains why a cat strains on the litter tray, or is constantly going in and out of it. In all cases, get to the vets as soon as you can.

4 BREATHING PROBLEMS

Unless they have been involved in a hectic play session with their favourite toy, cats breathe quietly, at a steady pace and with their mouths shut. Therefore, if your cat is panting, wheezing, has shallow breathing or is having to breathe through their mouth, there could be lung issues or problems with their airways. Cats who are finding it difficult to breathe will often have to sleep in a different position to normal, possibly with their head and neck extended. Excessive sneezing and coughing can also be signs of respiratory problems and should be checked out.

5 FREQUENT VOMITING

It isn't unusual for a cat to vomit from time to time, either because of a hairball, because they have scoffed their food too quickly or because they have eaten something you'd really rather not know about. But if they are regularly being sick for more than two days, it could be a sign of liver disease, infection, intestinal problems or even cancer. If there is blood in the vomit, you definitely need a vet. It's worth noting that a cat who is vomiting for more than two days can suffer from dehydration, so get booked in at the vets.

Get in the habit of checking the colour of your cat's eyes, gums and skin. If they look pale, your cat could be anaemic; yellow is a sign of jaundice; and a blue cast can be lack of oxygen. In any case, contact the vet ASAP.

HOW TO KEEP YOUR CAT HAPPY

The very best ways to ensure that your fur baby stays happy, healthy and carefree

WORDS ELLA CARTER

KEEP THEM SAFE

Cats are territorial creatures and like to stay close to their home patch, but that's not to say that an adventure might not be tempting once in a while — especially while hunting. If they stray a little too far, ensure that you can be reunited quickly and easily by getting your cat microchipped and include an ID tag on their collar. That way, you're just a phone call away! Your vet can help with microchipping, which is a legal requirement for cat owners.

LET THEM SCRATCH

Cats love a good scratch! They do this for a number of different reasons, ranging from keeping their claws in top condition (the act of scratching removes any dead skin and any frayed outer claws, and helps sharp, new claws develop), to using scratching to mark their territory. And of course, it feels good and some cats just love it as a way to relax, or express emotion. Either way, cats instinctively need to do this, and will find a way to direct this energy onto the most scratchable thing, which, particularly for indoor cats, can often be your furniture!

To keep your cat satisfied and your furniture scratch-free, consider investing in a scratching post as a designated zone for this behaviour. This way you can keep your cat happy by providing what they need, and save your home from being slightly shredded by sharp kitty claws!

KEEP FLEAS AND TICKS AT BAY

Bugs and critters are never a good thing, and can cause irritation and spread disease — especially if your cat is a free-range hunter who likes to pursue adventure outdoors. This innate desire to roam can lead them into all sorts of different environments where there's the potential to pick up parasites, and so it's important to be prepared.

Your vet will be able to help you with the best advice on what's good for your cat, and prescribe flea, tick and worming medication. You need to keep on top of this and treat your cat regularly, to make sure that no nasties are brought home, keeping your furry friend in top condition.

It's also a good idea to routinely check your cat for bites and bugs too, just in case. Regular grooming with your cat will mean that any unwanted visitors can be removed quickly.

PROVIDE DELICIOUS, NUTRITIOUS FOOD

A tasty dinner is a sure-fire way to your cat's heart! Depending on your cat's preference for taste or whether it's wet or dry food (some cats can be fussy!), you need to ensure that you're feeding your cat a balanced diet with plenty of recommended nutrients that's appropriate for its age. You can supplement this with additional tasty training treats for a balanced diet.

KEEP THINGS FRESH

Another great way to keep your cat happy is to encourage regular playtime with a variety of different treats and toys. Cats love stimulation from different tastes and textures, and they'll also love the bonding time that you can spend together playing and training.

You don't need to spend money to do this – you can make cat toys out of all kinds of household materials (as long as they're safe) to keep your cat entertained, but if you do want to pamper your cat, monthly subscription boxes can be a great option to provide plenty of feline fun.

CHECK FOR STRESS

A happy cat will be relaxed and calm, often dozing and purring during downtime and alert and sharp when it's time to exercise or play. But just like us, cats can get anxious and stressed, so it's important to know how to recognise the signs of stress in your cat so that you can help them when they need you!

Stress can show in many ways in your cat – but the best way to recognise it is to be aware of any out-of-the-ordinary signs. Maybe your cat is eating, drinking or toileting differently. Or perhaps they're skittish or scared more, hiding frequently or showing any kind of aggression or obsessive behaviour like grooming too much.

If you notice any of these signs, the next step is to identify the cause and take steps to soothe your cat in their environment. Pheromone plug-ins can be really beneficial to keeping cats happy, as they mimic the chemicals produced by mother cats and territory marking that helps your kitty to feel safe and secure.

SUPPLY RUNNING WATER

Ever noticed that your cat might help itself to a taste of water from a dripping tap? This is because cats just love running water, as opposed to still water from a bowl. It's thought that this might be down to how cats would drink in the wild, opting for fresh running water rather than drinking from stagnant pools. It also could be due to this method being more comfortable than knocking sensitive whiskers on the side of a water bowl. If you really want to make your cat happy, consider treating them to a cat fountain. This is a little water fountain with a constant stream of water for your cat to lap from, which is the perfect feline hydration experience!

PROVIDE A TOP-NOTCH BIRD WATCHING SPOT

Keeping one eye on the outside while relaxing in the sun is the perfect cat pastime. Although it might seem like a mundane way to spend an afternoon to us, to our furry buddies looking out the window is a very stimulating activity. Cats are really curious creatures, and watching the goings on of garden birds, other cats, squirrels, dogs, insects and more is time very well spent for a cat. Couple this with a cosy, window-adjacent spot to snooze in, and that's one happy cat.

Placing a nice bed next to a window will make your cat the happiest ever! Or why not go one step further and invest in a special cat hammock to ensure that window-gazing is as luxurious as possible?

GIVE THEM EXERCISE

Just like every other animal, cats need exercise to thrive. Whether it's hunting, chasing, running or a sudden burst of the zoomies triggered by excess energy, excitement or a trip to the litter box – exercise of all kinds is stimulating and fun for cats. It's also essential for maintaining a healthy weight.

If your furry friends are house cats, this can be harder to encourage, and so the best way to keep cats fit and happy is to play with them for around 30 minutes a day (but every cat is different!). If they need a bit more exercise, there are even specialist cat treadmills that can help your furbabies let off some steam!

PROVIDE A NICE, PRIVATE LITTER TRAY

Taking care of basic needs will ensure that your cat is happy and relaxed. It's important to put your cat's essential resources in key places throughout your home so that they're happy with the placement – and if you have an indoor cat – or a cat that doesn't do its business outside – this includes the litter tray. It's important to think about where you place this, as it's where cats can feel most vulnerable. Place one out of the way of children and other pets, in a quiet part of your home where they won't be disturbed. This will help your cat stay mentally content, and will mean that they won't seek out other places in your house that suit their toileting habits better!

You could consider a covered litter tray, which gives your cat a quiet and private space and means that there's no mess if your cat likes to dig afterwards! However some cats don't like these, so you may have to try a few things before the perfect option presents itself.

LET THEM CLIMB

Getting up high is something that cats crave – it helps them survey their environment, scan for predators and provide a feeling of safety and security. This is because cats are both predators and prey and so they prefer to be on the lookout and out of harm's way.

To help with this love of climbing, you can provide a freestanding cat tree to provide some height, but if you want to go all out – try installing catwalks or a cat playground in your home! This consists of little platforms or bridges (or even tunnels) mounted high on the walls, to allow cats the freedom to play and relax up high. The sky is the limit for what you can do!

STOCK UP ON PREY TOYS

Hunting is a key instinct for your furry friend. They're hardwired to want to stalk and pounce, and they love to do this during playtime as well as for real. Make the time to get involved in the process – it is a great way to have fun and bond with your cat. You can buy or easily make prey-style toys to dangle or drag along the floor and let your cat chase. Think about feathers, bells and other delicate prey-style things that will catch your cat's attention and lure them into the fun! Just make sure there isn't anything they can swallow.

SNUGGLE

If they like it, one of the best ways to keep your cat happy is to have a good cuddle session. Despite appearing to be aloof and individual for the majority of their day, there will probably be time when your cat wants to be close with you. Kittens seek out this closeness from their mum to feel safe, warm and protected, and adult cats take this behaviour into later life. Just remember to not squeeze too hard – and add in a gentle chin scratch for extra purrs.

YOUR CAT'S FAVOURITE THINGS

From tasty treats to toasty naps in sunny places, there are some things that no cat can resist!

WORDS ELLA CARTER

1 HEIGHTS
Ever noticed that your cat just loves to be up high? They'll find the top of cabinets or shelves to snooze on, or scramble up trees to observe their environment from a loft vantage point. This is an instinctual behaviour that enables your cat to both survey for prey, and keep an eye out for any would-be predators.

2 GROOMING
One of your cat's favourite pastimes is grooming – cats are super clean creatures and can spend up to 50 percent of their waking day doing this. It's as much for cleaning and conditioning their coat as it is for removing dirt and smell to mask from their prey. But it is also for bonding – your cat will love for you to get involved!

3 SUNNY SPOTS
A snooze in the sun is the ultimate catnap! This is an efficient way for cats to regulate their temperature during sleeping, and they will often track the path of the sun to find a toasty spot.

4 PLAYTIME
A playful cat is a happy cat and just like us, there's nothing better than letting off some steam and expending some energy. Chasing lasers, stalking toy mice and batting balls – playing triggers your cat's hunting instincts and they just can't resist. This also keeps things interesting and fun for your cat, plus playing together is a great way to bond.

"PLAYING TRIGGERS YOUR CAT'S HUNTING INSTINCTS"

5 HUNTING
If playtime is hunting practice, then this is the real deal – and if your cat is an outdoor hunter, they'll love flexing their predator muscles. Hunting comes naturally to cats and the thrill of the chase is definitely up there with their favourite pastimes. What's not necessarily ideal is the little presents that come with it, but try to look happy for your cat's sake!

6 PLACES TO HIDE
Curling up in boxes, under beds or in specially purchased luxury cat caves is one of your cat's favourite ways to snooze. They love this because it helps them feel safe and secure, concealed from predators and ambush.

7 YOU!
You are undoubtedly one of your cat's favourite things! Especially if you play with them regularly, work on some training together and spend time getting to know each other – just being around you will make your cat feel relaxed and happy!

Playing with fun toys is irresistible fun for your kitty, who will instinctually practise their hunting skills

8 CATNIP
Cats can go crazy for catnip! It's a totally safe plant (that's actually a member of the mint family) that you can grow in your garden or buy from pet shops or in cat toys, and some cats just love to roll around in it as it triggers the 'happy' receptors in their brain. When cats eat it, they can also have different behaviour changes such as stretching, drooling, jumping and bursts of hyperactivity.

9 A BUDDY
Ever thought about getting your cat a friend? Even though they are solitary animals, cats can be social creatures and can co-exist happily with other cats and even become best friends.

10 TREATS
Chicken or fish? Your cat will happily go for both, as some delicious treats will absolutely be one of your cat's favourite things. Choose a variety of flavours and textures to keep things interesting, and mix them up during training to keep your kitty interested!

5 THINGS TO NEVER DO WITH A CAT

Be the best cat protector you can be by ensuring you never do any of the following to your feline friend

WORDS JO COLE

1 DON'T LOSE YOUR COOL

Cats are sensitive creatures with excellent hearing, so you need to tailor your behaviour accordingly. People flapping around and making lots of noise can frighten them, and being heavy-handed when petting can make a cat nervous. Never force attention onto a cat or stare at one, as this is perceived as a sign of aggression. When it comes to discipline, reward good behaviour instead of shouting at bad behaviour. The cat will have no idea why you are suddenly shouting, and could lose trust in you. Keep your household nice and serene – a calm human means a happy cat.

2 KNOW YOUR PLANTS

There are lots of indoor and outdoor plants that are safe for cats to nuzzle and lick and even have a cheeky chew on. But there are many more that are incredibly unsafe. While most will only harm if ingested, some will cause real damage from just the slightest interaction. Lilies are one example – every part of a lily is poisonous to a cat, so much so that even licking water that cut lilies have been stood in can cause kidney failure. There are plenty of online resources to help you discover the plants to avoid, so make sure you research before you buy.

3 DON'T LET YOUR CAT PLAY WITH YARN

Cats have often been depicted frantically chasing after balls of yarn, and although it's something they might enjoy, it's something you should never allow. Yarn, as well as string, can cause significant damage if your cat manages to swallow any. As the yarn makes its way through the intestines, it can get caught up, becoming what's known as a linear foreign body. The yarn can cause parts of the intestine to become knotted, those parts then die and have to be surgically removed. Stick to proper cat toys, and always supervise your cat when playing.

4 AVOID A DRY FOOD DIET

Cats, being the gloriously stubborn creatures they are, don't always feel an urge to drink when thirsty, or even if they are dehydrated. Thankfully a lot of the water a cat needs is provided by wet food. Although it's fine to give your cat some dry biscuits, just one wet meal a day can avoid a bunch of health issues caused by dehydration. And on the subject of what to feed your cat, don't try to give them a vegan diet. Cats are obligate carnivores, so not only are they physically unable to process plant-based food, meat provides certain components that are vital to their wellbeing.

5 DON'T SHAVE YOUR CAT

You might think you are helping your cat by trimming or shaving their fur, especially when it's baking hot, but it's something you should never, ever do. Cats need their fur in order to regulate their body temperature, so by shaving them you are actually doing serious harm. Unless a vet has to shave your cat for a medical reason, it's something they should never experience. Instead of reaching for the shaver, brush your cat regularly to remove excess fur and keep their coat in top condition.

Stick to toys that won't harm your cat instead of letting them play with a ball of yarn, which could be dangerous

"NEVER FORCE ATTENTION ON TO A CAT OR STARE"

Most cats are lactose intolerant, so don't give them cow's milk or other dairy products. In fact, never feed them human food unless you have checked it's safe for felines.

Image © Getty Images

BREED BEHAVIOUR

Take a prowl into the world of feline characteristics, where each breed has its own unique traits, demands and drive to play

WORDS BEE GINGER

Cats and humans alike thrive on respect and attention, but most of all love. What you put into your relationship with your feline you will get back in spades

Like its paw print, each cat is an individual. However, their personalities, appearance and often their behaviour can vary greatly. A cat's environment and genetic make up also plays a part in how they behave and react to the surroundings and humans in their lives. So what matters more when it comes to a cat's personality: nurture or nature? Could it all be down to their breed?

Unlike dog breeds, cat breeds are not as easy to discern, but there are many different ones other than your good old moggy, all of which have unique needs and a wide range of characteristics.

"LIKE ITS PAW PRINT, EACH CAT IS AN INDIVIDUAL"

FIVE FELINE PERSONALITY TRAITS

The American Veterinary Medical Association conducted a number of studies in which it found five main feline personality traits (not including hiding surprises in your shoes). These studies applied to both indoor and outdoor cats and cats of all breeds, however, the breeds can further be split into two broad categories of more relaxed breeds, and more adventurous breeds.

IMPULSIVE This includes recklessness and erraticism (and could possibly account for that daily mad cat half hour!).

EXTRAVERSION These traits include inquisitiveness, curiosity (which hopefully didn't kill the cat), being vigilant and inventive.

AGREEABLE Gentleness, affection and friendliness towards people all fall under this category.

DOMINANCE This is often directed at other cats and can manifest as aggression and dominance as well as bullying.

NEUROTICISM This section encompasses shyness, anxiety, suspicion and possible fearfulness around humans and other animals.

FAMILY-FRIENDLY CATS

A house is not a home without a cat

We can all agree that a cat is a great addition to a family. They bring fun and warmth to a home and are a great companion for young and old alike. But some breeds are better suited to a family's busy lifestyle, especially one with small children and other animals. A feline friend is not only a splendid keeper of secrets and an excellent snuggle buddy for children, but an important addition for teaching them responsibility and patience.

When choosing a cat, it is wise to consider the activity level and age of all the family members to determine which feline would make the purr-fect fit; a crazy kitten or a slightly more sedate lady of the manor. The American Shorthair, for example, is a breed well-suited to families and children in particular. These sturdy little guys are low-maintenance and get along with other animals, and with a history as working cats they can help out around the home by catching vermin!

> "SOME BREEDS ARE BETTER SUITED TO A FAMILY'S BUSY LIFE"

Birmans are affectionate cats but can become jealous if they aren't paid enough attention

The American Shorthair is an all-round great family cat with a sweet and relaxed temperament that tends to live a long life

CATS ABOUT THE HOUSE
- Birman
- Ragdoll
- Maine Coon
- Manx
- Himalayan
- European Burmese
- Abyssinian

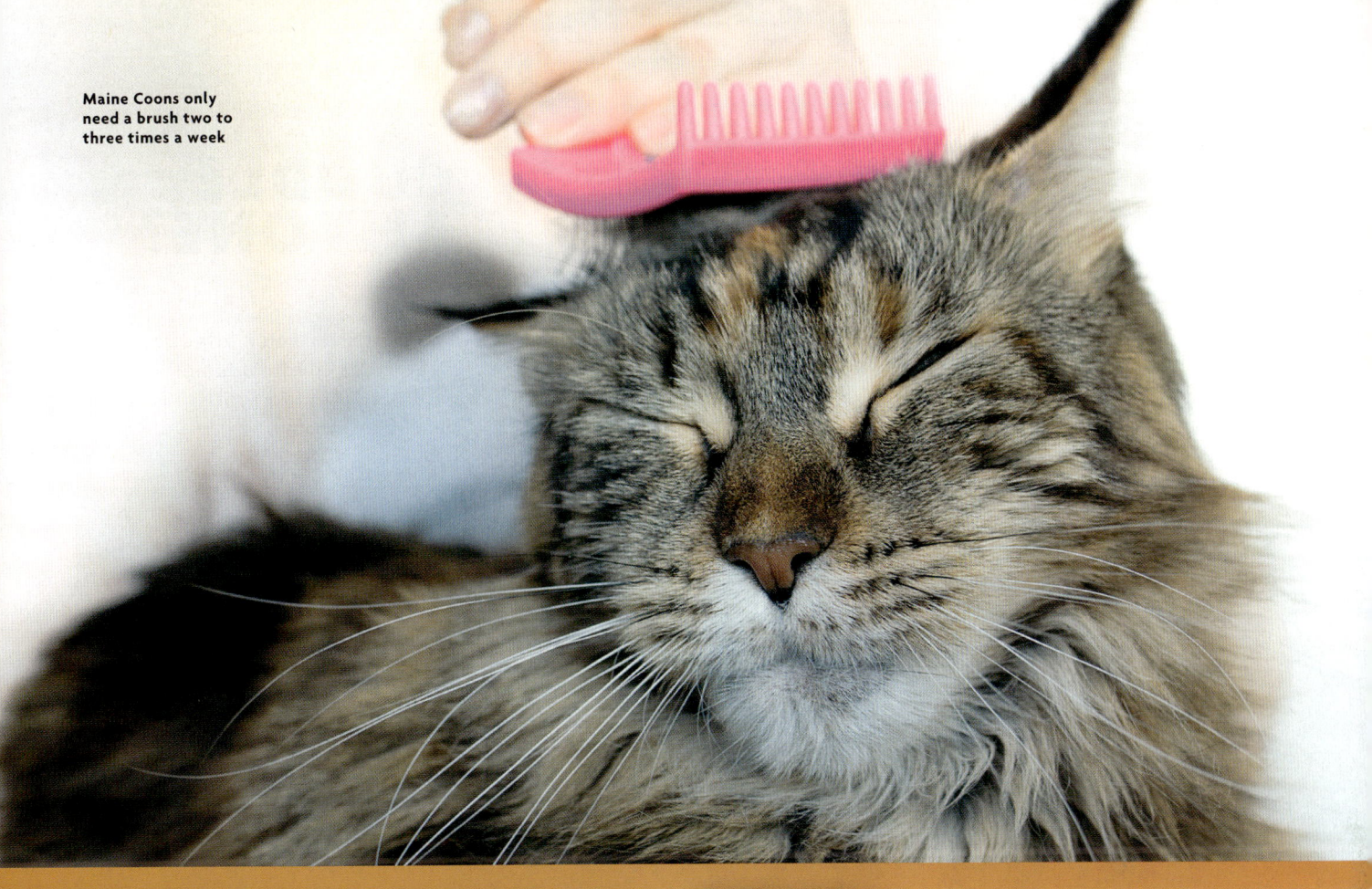

Maine Coons only need a brush two to three times a week

Minimal grooming is needed for the Burmese's silky coat

THESE CATS HAVE THEIR OWN GROOMING ROUTINE

- Burmese
- Korat
- Devon Rex
- Siamese
- European Burmese
- Havana Brown
- Turkish Angora

EASY TO GROOM

Some furry companions aren't reliant on their humans to look their best

Cats are known to take pride in their appearance and spend a large amount of time grooming themselves. However, every feline appreciates a little help in the grooming department from time to time, although some kitties are easier to groom than others. There are breeds whose coats can be cared for with minimal maintenance as they all have short hair, which makes them easy to brush. Grooming should not be a stressful undertaking and sessions should be kept to just five or ten minutes. Try to pick a time when your cat is already calm and sleepy, such as after dinner.

A gentle brush coupled with some stroking can be enough to send your furry (or not-so-furry) friend to sleep

AFFECTIONATE CATS

These four-legged companions absolutely love to snuggle up

To anyone who doesn't live with (or – perish the thought – like) cats, it can seem as though they are aloof, cold and unaffectionate pets, but this couldn't be further from the truth. There are many ways in which cats express their love towards humans, but affection does have to be earned. However, there are some breeds who will offer affection more willingly.

A cat will let you know it trusts you (the ultimate compliment) by rolling over to expose its tummy, backing its rear into you, licking you and rubbing its cheeks against you (thereby releasing pheromones from the glands located on its cheeks).

Other acts of love can come in the form of head bunting (rubbing heads), purring, nibbling, tail twitches and leaving you 'gifts' in the shape of dead animals, something that your cat has dedicated time and energy to catching just to share its prize with you. To a predator there can be no greater sign of friendship.

A cat's tummy is its most vulnerable part, so by exposing it to you it's letting you know it feels safe around you

Licking is a sign that your cat trusts you

CUDDLE ANYONE?

SCOTTISH FOLD
These cats thrive on affection and make great cuddle buddies and lap cats. All purebred Scottish Folds are descended from one cat – a white barn puss named Susie.

RAGDOLL
This breed not only has the cutest name but also a docile and affectionate temperament and they love spending plenty of time with humans. They might look cute and dainty, but Ragdolls can weigh as much as nine kilograms.

BALINESE
These cats love to sit quietly and be petted by their humans. Although they are known for their inquisitive nature and intelligence they make for the best companions. The Balinese cat doesn't actually have any ancestral links to Bali – or anywhere in Indonesia for that matter.

A rescue cat from Devon is the current owner of the loudest purr on record. In 2015, 13-year-old Merlin was recorded purring at 67.8 decibels, 43 decibels louder than the average cat!

WE NEED ATTENTION!

- Balinese-Javanese
- Burmese
- Oriental
- Tonkinese
- Singapura
- Peterbald

MOUTHY MAMMALS

Cats have perfected the art of meowing to get what they want

The pitch, length and tone of a meow will differ depending on what your cat is trying to tell you

It may not seem like it when your cat wakes you up meowing for breakfast, but vocalising doesn't come naturally to cats. Rather, they've had to learn to do so in order to communicate with humans. By developing a series of vocalisations, cats are able to get our attention, ensuring we recognise and then meet their needs, whether they are demanding a fresh bowl of food, a cuddle on the sofa or would like to bring a dirty litter tray to your attention. And certain breeds are very chatty catties.

Some studies have even suggested that cats have learned to meow at a similar pitch to a human baby, thereby cleverly stimulating our natural instincts to nurture and protect. They really have got us humans wrapped around their paws!

"CATS HAVE LEARNED TO MEOW AT A SIMILAR PITCH TO A HUMAN BABY"

HIGH-MAINTENANCE MOGGIES

From unique ailments to daily brushing, some breeds require a lot of attention

Cats generally have the reputation of being a pretty low-maintenance pet. They exercise themselves and bathe regularly, wash other family members and can catch their own food if needed. Some of the more unusual breeds, however, can be more of a challenge when it comes to being looked after. The care needs of individual cats will vary, but in the case of purebreds in particular, many external factors need to be taken into consideration, as they have unique health, dietary, grooming and behavioural issues that can pose more of an issue.

> "SOME BREEDS CAN BE MORE OF A CHALLENGE"

While most breeds will take care of their own hygiene routine, some need help to keep themselves healthy

SERVICE!

HIMALAYAN
The Himalayan needs daily grooming to remove tangles from their long hair. They can suffer with breathing issues due to deformed nasal passages, which are common among flat-faced cats. They're also at risk of polycystic kidney disease as they age.

MANX
The Manx is easily identified by the absence of a tail and, over the years, has become a fashionable breed. As with any breeding abnormality, the breed's taillessness can be associated with spinal defects that can present as problems defecating or urinating. Most of these problems appear by six months of age. A Manx kitten likely has some spinal issue if they are displaying difficulty walking or walk with a stiff or hopping gait.

SPHYNX
Among the most unusual cats in appearance, the Sphynx cat is virtually hairless. Before you get too excited by the fact that this feline won't need daily grooming, you should be aware that the breed does face some challenges. Sphynxes are prone to hypertrophic cardiomyopathy (a thickening of the heart muscle) and a neurological disease called hereditary myopathy, which affects the muscles (including the ability to swallow). Fortunately, the latter condition is rare and is being slowly bred out. Sphynx cats are also prone to some skin conditions, as well as periodontal disease. So yes, you'll have to brush their teeth.

Cats are clever enough to have learned how to open doors and even use a toilet

Cats can comprehend what other animals of different species (including humans) are communicating to them

CANNY CATS

Your feline friend is a highly intelligent animal capable of learning tricks and commands

We all know that cats can be crafty creatures, but they might be cleverer than many of us appreciate. Studies have found that an adult cat possesses the same mental capacity as a two-year-old human child. Science has also uncovered that, like ours, cats' brains comprise individual, interconnected specialised sections that enable them to study, interact with and manipulate their environment. Cats also have object permanence recognition, meaning they understand that just because something disappears from view it doesn't mean that it no longer exists.

If all this wasn't proof enough of how clever cats are, they have been shown to understand and remember certain commands such as "sit" and "fetch", open closed doors and even learn to use a toilet.

WISE OLD WHISKERS

ABYSSINIAN
This smart feline consistently tops the list for the most intelligent cat breed, one known to relish racing around agility courses. There is evidence to suggest that, despite its name, the Abyssinian may in fact have originated in Egypt.

SIAMESE
Not only do these cats crave mental stimulation in the form of puzzle toys, but if they get bored they will start turning the taps on around the house! A Thai book of cat poems written between the 14th and 18th centuries depicts Siamese cats, indicating that the breed could be at least over 200 years old.

BENGAL
Similar to its Siamese counterpart, the Bengal will amuse itself if you don't; they have a penchant for switching lights on and off. The Bengal is a relatively young breed in the cat world. It wasn't accepted by The International Cat Association until 1983.

IT'S PLAY TIME!

Whether they are a kitten or a senior member of the family, all cats need to play

Cats enjoy playing for a variety of reasons, from fending off boredom to unleashing their predatory instincts. Play is especially important for kittens as it helps them to socialise with other cats and hone skills they will need later on in life. But play isn't restricted to the carefree days of rolling about with the rest of the litter; cats of all ages enjoy regular games, which offer a fun form of exercise (thereby avoiding weight gain) and a way to bond with their humans. Different cats will prefer different games, with some loving nothing more than pouncing on a toy mouse, while others take the time to work out a puzzle toy in order to reach a tasty reward inside.

> "PLAY IS ESPECIALLY IMPORTANT FOR KITTENS AS IT HELPS THEM TO SOCIALISE"

It's crucial that you regularly make time to play with your cat. It will keep them happy and help to strengthen your bond

Birmas have a high play drive and love venturing outside

FELINE ACTIVE

- Birma
- Maine Coon
- Devon Rex
- Munchkin
- Manx
- Siberian Forest
- Turkish Angora

Cats rarely travel further than 400m, preferring to stay near, maybe scaling a tree in your garden

Not all cats will have the temperament for it, but some are fine with travelling long distances

OUT AND ABOUT

- Turkish Van
- American Bobcat
- Ocicat
- Persian
- Somali
- American Shorthair

Agile and inquisitive, there are few places that cats won't explore

CURIOSITY THRILLED THE CAT

Most cats love to go exploring, but they might not roam as far as you'd think

Cats are curious by nature, and virtually all felines are adventurous to a degree. Driven by the urge to hunt (regardless of whether you've just fed them a juicy portion of cat food) and explore their surroundings, cats will often prowl the neighbourhood at dawn and dusk, but studies have revealed that most never venture further than 400 metres from home. Some more daring souls will range between one and three kilometres, but this is really only common among males and farm cats.

Whether your cat occasionally scales the tree at the end of your garden or regularly disappears for hours at a time, it's very important to allow them to follow their natural compulsion to wander.

"DRIVEN BY THE URGE TO HUNT, CATS WILL OFTEN PROWL AT DAWN AND DUSK"

KID-LOVING CATS

A laid-back, loving cat makes for great company for children

Cats are sensitive, alert and extremely susceptible to loud noises, sudden changes and strange smells. With all that considered, you'd think the last thing a cat would want to be around is a child, but that really isn't the case. In fact, cats can be the perfect companion for children and help them to learn crucial life lessons.

Aside from being great playmates, the presence of a cat can teach children to be empathetic and patient. A cat must be cared for and handled gently, but a child's instinct will be to chase it and perhaps cuddle it too roughly. This can upset the cat and result in the child getting scratched. Instead, by being shown by an adult how to behave around a cat, a child will learn to temper their natural urges and do what is best for the animal.

Another benefit of having cats around is they boost children's immune systems and help to fend off respiratory problems, including asthma, later on in life.

Growing up with animals teaches children about responsibility and caring for others

Children can learn empathy from bonding with a cat

Keeping a cat as a pet can have health benefits for kids

CHILD-FRIENDLY

RAGAMUFFIN

These easy-going, laid-back cats are ideal for people living in an apartment and benefit from having a regular play time. The origins of the word 'ragamuffin' are unclear, but in the 19th century children in the US would dress up for 'ragamuffin parades' in which they wandered around begging for their Thanksgiving meal.

AMERICAN SHORTHAIR

This loyal and loving breed enjoys the company of both people and other animals and has no objections to being picked up for a cuddle. Transported across the Atlantic to the US in the 1600s, the Shorthair was once used to keep vermin away from grain fields

MAINE COON

This large breed is known for its canine-like qualities, making it a very affectionate, patient and loyal pet. The Maine Coon is known as 'the gentle giant' of cats.

5 THINGS YOUR CAT WANTS YOU TO KNOW

As much as we'd all love to be Dr Dolittles, it's just not possible to communicate with our cats verbally. There are, however, other ways...

WORDS NATALIE DENTON

1 I DON'T SHARE
The introduction of a new feline into the home might stress or anger your cat. If it starts hiding, doing its business outside the litter box, takes to spraying around the house or being more destructive than normal, it's telling you that it wants the new cat out.

2 COMFORT ME
Cats will come to you when they want comfort. Usually they'll bunt your legs or hand, curl their tail around you, or arch their body in a non-aggressive way (soft, curled tail), inviting you to pet them.

3 I'M NOT HAPPY WITH MY BED
If your cat isn't sleeping where you'd like it to or usually does, it's not telling you it wants a new bed – the opposite in fact. It wants the bed to go back to how it was, probably before you washed it or someone else touched or moved it.

4 THERE'S A PROBLEM WITH MY FOOD
Generally speaking cats aren't picky eaters, so if your cat stops eating the same food it has had for a while, it's probably not that it's got bored of it, it could be that it's developed a problem digesting the food.

5 I DON'T NEED FRIENDS
If you go to cuddle your cat and it moves away, it's a big no. If it growls, hisses or spits then it's either scared, angry, or just plain ticked off. If their ears are flat and back, the tail and fur up, and perhaps worst of all, they've arched, step away from your cat.

YOUR CAT'S PET HATES

From pungent smells to old food and even inflatables, here are the things that really get on your cat's whiskers

WORDS BEE GINGER

As arguably one of the most upfront domesticated animals around, cats aren't exactly shy when it comes to letting us know what they like. From snuggling up for a cuddle to rolling around with soft toys and tucking into some fresh food, if a cat is content, you will know about it.

However, the same can't always be said for a cat that is in distress, uncomfortable or feeling threatened. While they do have an array of signals that they can use to express their displeasure, sometimes a situation is too overwhelming and a cat will seek to hide from whatever is upsetting them, often making it difficult for us humans to realise that they have disappeared for a reason.

Here are eight of the biggest things your cat loathes, so you can ensure that your environment is free of these triggers.

"IF A CAT IS CONTENT, YOU WILL KNOW ABOUT IT. THE SAME CAN'T BE SAID FOR A CAT IN DISTRESS"

Your cat will already be stressed out by an unexpected car journey, so try to avoid worsening the situation with a fuel stop

CERTAIN SMELLS

Cats navigate the world around them through a variety of senses, but none is more important than their sense of smell. Equipped with 200 million odour sensors in their noses (humans only have 5 million), cats can smell 14 times better than we can, which makes them highly susceptible to potent smells. The worst culprits include onions, vinegar, mint, lavender, rosemary, cinnamon and citrus fruits, the latter being so repugnant to cats that many companies have developed citrus-infused cat-repellents. It's also worth noting that cats loathe the smell of gasoline, so if you need to take them to the vet, ensure that you have already topped up your fuel so that you don't need to stop en route and expose your feline to a smell they hate.

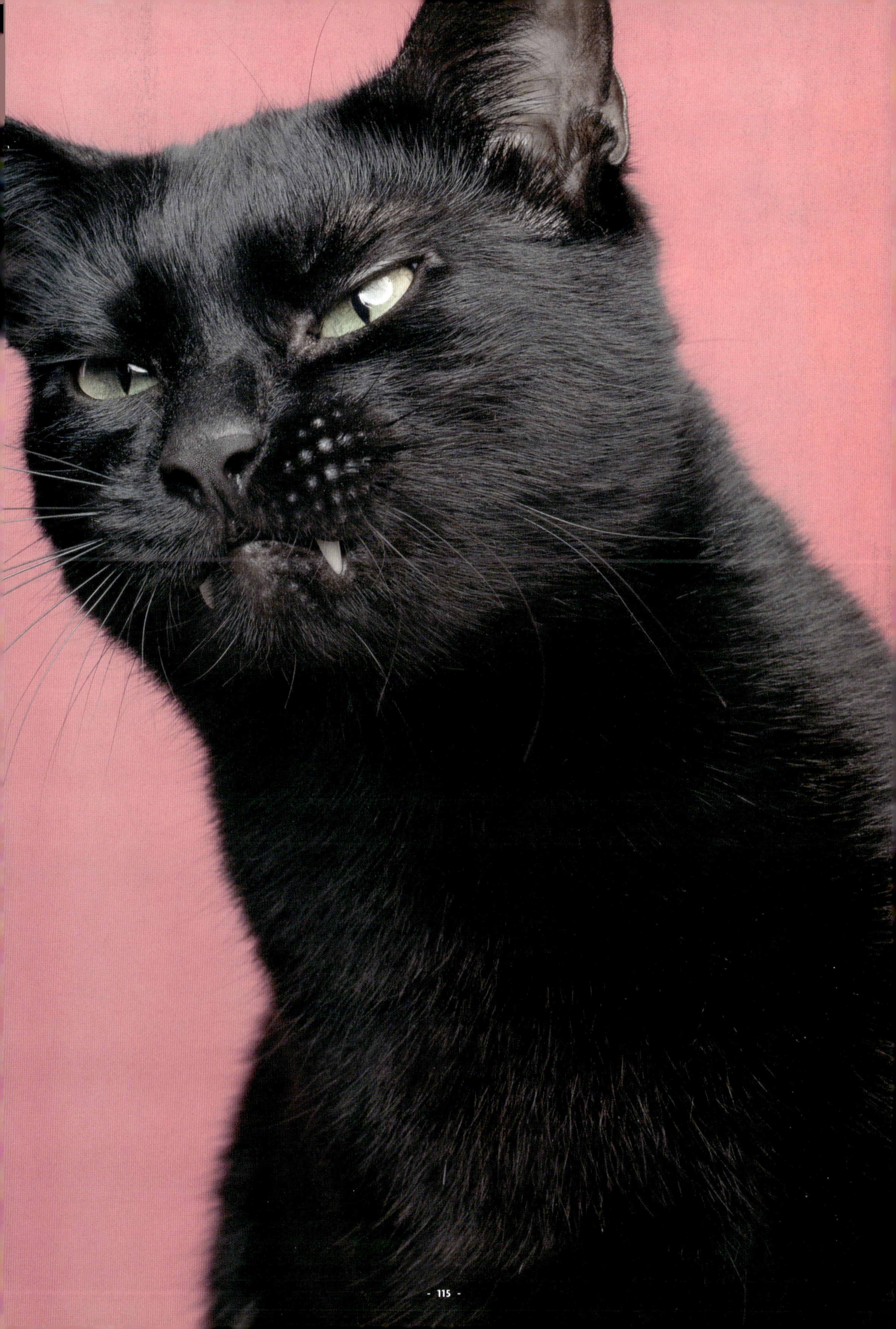

If you are going to put balloons up, avoid putting them where your cat is likely to hide or want to sleep

BALLOONS

Ah, the balloon. An innocent reminder of chaotic childhood birthday parties. An indication of an evening of fun and festivities ahead. No matter how old we are, balloons only ever mean a good time. Unfortunately, to our feline friends, they represent something entirely different. To a cat, a balloon is a helium-filled floating menace that cannot be overcome. What's more, they have a propensity to explode loudly.

Cats can't understand what these floating things are, and to them a balloon could be a threat to their safety or that of their family, and because balloons will be out of their reach, this rubbery imposter cannot be defeated and disposed of, unlike a mouse or insect. Cats pick fights that they can win, and when it comes to balloons they don't have many options but to run and hide.

LOUD NOISES

A sudden loud noise can make anybody jump, but usually once we ascertain the cause of it our heart rate begins to return to normal and we calm down. Unfortunately for cats, this process takes a lot longer and can inflict incredible stress and anxiety.

Cats can hear at pitches that elude even dogs, so a loud noise to you is utterly deafening to them. On top of that, a cat won't necessarily understand where the noise is coming from or what's causing it, scrambling with its instincts. How can a cat know where to run if it can't work out where the danger is?

Prolonged exposure to loud noises, such as raised voices, music or fireworks, can cause a cat to become skittish, aggressive or even depressed, which can in turn be followed by hair loss. For a cat to feel like it is in control of its surroundings, its home must be quiet, calm and familiar.

To us, watching fireworks is an enjoyable experience. To a cat it's a seemingly endless series of unpredictable noises that they don't understand

"I keep myself clean, human – I don't need a bath!"

WATER

It's no secret that, aside from a few breeds, cats almost universally despise water. But why? Some scientists believe it's all to do with how cats first evolved. While big cats such as tigers and jaguars emerged in climates that boast plenty of water sources in the form of rivers and lakes (which are rather usefully home to plenty of prey), the ancestors of the modern house cat prowled drier lands and therefore rarely – if ever – encountered a vast body of water. As a result cats developed a suspicion of an element that they almost never interacted with, and therefore they naturally choose to avoid it where possible.

Another reason for their hatred of the wet stuff is the fact that it weighs their coat down and makes them smell unfamiliar. Cats can detect the chemicals in water, so when they are drenched in it they instantly find that their own fur smells strange and they can't move as freely – two pretty upsetting developments for an animal that spends so much time grooming its coat and relies on speed to both catch prey and evade predators.

STALE FOOD

Here's one problem that your cat is likely to be very good at bringing up with you. Unlike dogs, who will devour almost anything given the chance, cats are extremely choosy about their food, and they must be served fresh food every day. If you notice that your cat is picking at its food then it's trying to let you know that it's either past its best or they don't like the flavour. Either way, no amount of cajoling is going to convince your cat to eat it, so you'd be better off finding them something else.

It's important for your cat's health that it is fed fresh food on a daily basis

HEAVY-HANDED PETTING

Gently petting and stroking your cat is a crucial part of bonding with them, one that has been scientifically proven to release endorphins in humans (thereby relieving stress and just generally making us feel good) and one that also helps to make your cat feel relaxed (being stroked feels similar to being nuzzled and groomed by another cat).

However, as highly sensitive animals, cats won't tolerate rough petting or handling. You must remain conscious at all times of where you are stroking your cat and heed any signals of discomfort that they give. All cats are different, and while some will happily roll over for a tummy rub, others will tear your hand to pieces if you so much as lay a finger on their belly.

Another thing to consider is your cat's ability to move freely. It's very important that you don't hold onto your cat too tightly or put your hands in their face. They need to know that, should a threat suddenly materialise, they will be able to react to it and stay safe.

We don't enjoy having our movement restricted, and neither does a cat. If they do feel trapped they could lash out

LONELINESS

We all appreciate some 'me' time every now and again, and cats are no exception. Being left in peace for a few hours' sleep makes for a content and healthy cat. However, while cats feel safest in a calm, quiet environment that they know well, they don't like being left alone for too long. This is because, despite their independent ways, cats form strong bonds with their owners, and when they are left for too long they can become anxious and even depressed. This can then manifest in them scratching too much, meowing excessively and following you everywhere when you are around. As a rough guide, a cat aged under four months shouldn't be left for more than four hours, while a cat aged six months or more should be okay for around eight hours by themselves. A fully grown and settled cat can be left for up to 48 hours at a time — only if you have no other choice.

They might be independent creatures, but that doesn't mean cats don't suffer from separation anxiety

If your cat runs away to hide from a new person in your home, it is best that they are left alone until they are ready to emerge

STRANGERS

It's natural to be wary of strangers, especially so when your safety depends on being given sufficient time to smell and observe them. This is the dilemma that all cats face when they meet a person for the first time. As highly territorial animals, cats find it disturbing when a stranger enters their world with new smells and signals that they have not had the time to explore. They like to feel completely in control of their surroundings, and the presence of someone unknown can therefore throw them completely. While some cats will overcome their reservations fairly quickly, others will take their time, perhaps even hiding for a while. The best thing to do is let them introduce themselves when they feel ready, instead of trying to force them to be sociable when they might be feeling anxious or unsettled.

Equipped with an incredibly sensitive nose and hearing beyond that of even dogs, cats can detect the most subtle changes in their environment

"THEIR ARSENAL INCLUDES A SENSE OF SMELL 14-TIMES STRONGER THAN OURS"

YOUR CAT'S SIXTH SENSE

From a storm rumbling in the distance to the Earth's vibrations and even impending death, our feline friends often seem to know what's going on long before we do

WORDS BEE GINGER

Ever since the first cats prowled the dusty plains of the Middle East, the need to remain alert and tuned in to their surroundings was imperative for avoiding predators and locating sufficient prey. Cats therefore evolved a series of biological advantages that enabled them first to survive and then to thrive in the wild. Their arsenal includes ears that can hear up to 64,000 hertz (approximately three-times higher than humans), eyes that can detect up to six- to eight-times more than ours in the dark, and a sense of smell 14-times stronger than a human's. In essence, they are perfectly engineered to pick up on even the slightest alteration in their environment. But it's not just changes in the weather, unusual smells or shifts in the atmosphere that cats are able to detect. It's now thought that they are able to sniff out disease, sense a looming natural disaster and even know when someone is about to die. Here are five remarkable things that your furry warning system can see coming well before you even realise something is afoot.

EARTHQUAKES
To humans it seems that earthquakes strike without warning, but cats can sense them coming and know when to run for cover

If you ever find yourself in a known earthquake hotspot and you notice a distinct lack of cats around, it might be an idea to seek shelter. This is because cats possess a knack for knowing when things are about to get seriously shaky.

Although hard proof has yet to be obtained, there is strong anecdotal evidence that cats can feel the vibrations emitted when the Earth's tectonic plates move, and according to a study conducted by German scientist Helmut Tributsch in the 1980s, they may even be able to detect the ions created when the Earth shifts.

If this wasn't enough, another experiment also undertaken in the 1980s, this time by a geologist, accurately predicted quakes in California by recording the number of missing pet adverts in the local newspapers. Jim Berkland rightly concluded that animals were fleeing their homes in search of safety far away from where the earthquakes would strike.

Footage of cats in a shop in Japan running for cover a few seconds before an earthquake occurred has convinced many viewers the animals knew what was coming

Storms
This is why your cat will rarely ever get caught in a downpour

We humans are forever getting caught in the rain, but while we run for cover, cursing our lack of umbrella as we go, we can be fairly confident that our feline friends are snuggled up warm and dry inside. This is because cats are able to detect the changes in temperature and atmospheric pressure that precede a storm. They can also sniff out the distinct smell of rain and hear the distant rumble of thunder long before we even know a storm is brewing. All of these tools inform cats of when it's time to search for cover, which, in an age before domestication and the comfort of a human home to hide in, would have been a vital piece of information.

Don't worry about the weather forecast – watching your cat's behaviour is just as good an indicator of a coming storm

FEAR
Cats are masters at instantly knowing when a human is scared

When we are scared or distressed our bodies release pheromones in our sweat. This instinctive response evolved so that humans could detect fear in others, a helpful warning sign for our ancient ancestors who lived in small, tight groups and relied on each other for survival. Another species that can smell our fear pheromones is cats, hardly surprising given that they can smell so much better than we can. Cats use our scent combined with our body language and tone of voice to rapidly piece together how we are feeling. But this impressive ability isn't just limited to fear; cats can tell when we are happy, sad or displaying a range of emotions.

When cats interact with a new object or person they will often look to their owners to gauge how they should behave. If you're fearful, your cat will be too

IMPENDING DEATH

Doctors and nurses can only ever guess when someone is close to the end, but it appears that cats know precisely when someone is about to pass away

Predicting when a terminally ill person is going to die is not an exact science, and despite all the progress made in the field of medicine, it's likely it will always remain this way. That is, unless we start to enlist the help of cats more often, for it appears that they can in fact sense death with uncanny accuracy.

In 2007 a cat named Oscar gained a reputation for knowing when patients being cared for in a dementia ward in Providence, Rhode Island, were about to breathe their last. Sensing a patient's end looming, Oscar would head into their room, jump up on their bed and settle down for a cuddle. If at any point a member of staff or visitor removed him from the room, he would scratch and meow at the door until he was permitted to come back in. On at least 25 occasions (some accounts say as many as 50) the recipient of Oscar's affections would pass away within a few hours of his visit.

While there is no conclusive evidence, it's thought that Oscar was able to smell the chemicals being released by the dying patients, something that our noses are not strong enough to pick up.

Aside from Oscar, there have also been reports of a cat acting similarly towards dying patients in a care home in Australia

IT'S A BLUR

Contrary to popular belief, cats don't see in as much detail as we do. This is due to an evolutionary trade-off between their need to spot movement quickly (such as when a mouse passes by) and being able to see things in fine detail. It's far more important for a cat to be able to notice prey (or a predator) and react to it than it is for the cat to be able to see the different layers in a mouse's fur, for instance. So something that we can see in fine detail at 30 metres (100 feet) away would be a blur to a cat, which would only be able to see it properly at around six metres (20 feet) away.

CANCER

If your cat suddenly starts paying particular attention to a part of you it might be time for a check up

There is increasing evidence to suggest that cats (like dogs) can detect cancer in humans, helping to alert them to a potentially serious problem before it gets any worse. Although this hasn't been proven scientifically, there are numerous reports of cats pawing at a particular part of their owner (such as a breast) or insisting on snuggling up to an area where cancer was later found. It's also thought that cats may be able to recognise the early warning signs before a diabetic suffers a hypoglycemic episode.

Scientists still aren't sure if cats can 'smell' cancer cells

BENEFITS OF HAVING A CAT

Cats are so much more than just pets. Welcoming a feline into your family has hidden benefits that range from rodent repulsion to heart health

WORDS LAURA MEARS

1 THEY REDUCE ALLERGIES
A 2019 research study from Finland showed that exposure to cats in early life reduces childrens' risk of eczema. Add dogs into the mix and the risk of asthma and other allergies drops too.

2 THEY SAVE LIVES
In England, a cat called Pixie alerted its owners when their toddler started choking in the night. In Indiana, a cat called Peanut Buster woke their owner when the house was on fire. And in Russia, a cat called Crimean Tom saved troops from starvation by leading them to hidden food.

3 THEY HEAL INJURIES
According to The Journal of the Acoustical Society of America, a cat's purr might have healing properties! The sounds they make are at frequencies that can reduce pain and even help bones to heal.

4 THEY GIVE YOU PERMISSION TO PLAY
Attracted by the slightest of movements, even a senior feline will often jump at the chance of a chase. Having a cat at home gives you the perfect excuse to take a break from your busy day and rediscover your inner child. Attract your pet's attention with toys that mimic the size and movement of their natural prey.

5 THEY'RE GREAT COMPANY
According to a survey by Cats Protection, the main reason people own cats is as companions. Having a cat at home is a great way to reduce stress and combat loneliness.

6 THEY TAKE CARE OF THEMSELVES
Cats are much lower maintenance than dogs, giving you all the benefits of pet ownership for a fraction of the effort. They take themselves for a walk, have daily baths, and don't mind a little time alone while you're out at work. They're also much cheaper to feed and less likely to chew holes in your favourite slippers.

7 THEY SCARE RODENTS
Cats weren't always cuddly pets. When they first started living alongside humans, they were ruthless rodent-killers. As a result, mice evolved to fear our feline companions. Just the smell of a cat in the house can be enough to keep them away.

8 THEIR FRIENDSHIP CAN LAST DECADES
Cats live much longer than most other pets. The average hamster lasts just two years, a rabbit lives for nine years, and a dog for 12 years. But, if you're lucky, your cat could live for 20 years, giving you two whole decades of companionship, love, and affection.

9 **THEY PROTECT YOUR HEART**
A study by the University of Minnesota's Stroke Institute showed that cats might protect their owners' hearts. The decade-long experiment revealed that people with cats at home were a third less likely to die from a heart attack.

10 **THEY MAKE YOU LAUGH**
Cats do the funniest things, and their silly behaviour is good for your health. Laughing releases endorphins and reduces stress hormones, completely changing the chemistry of your body.

Your cat's purr might have healing properties

Spending time with your cat can lower stress and reduce loneliness

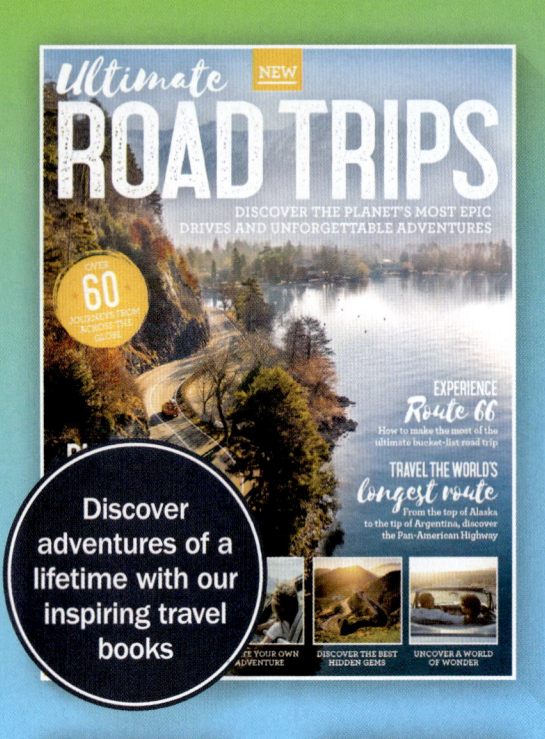

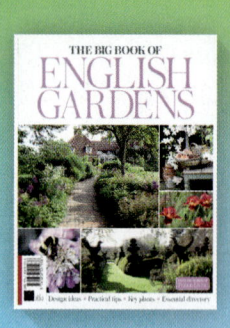

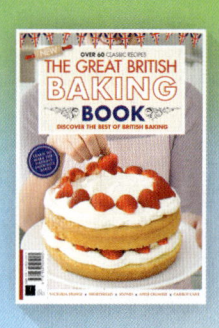

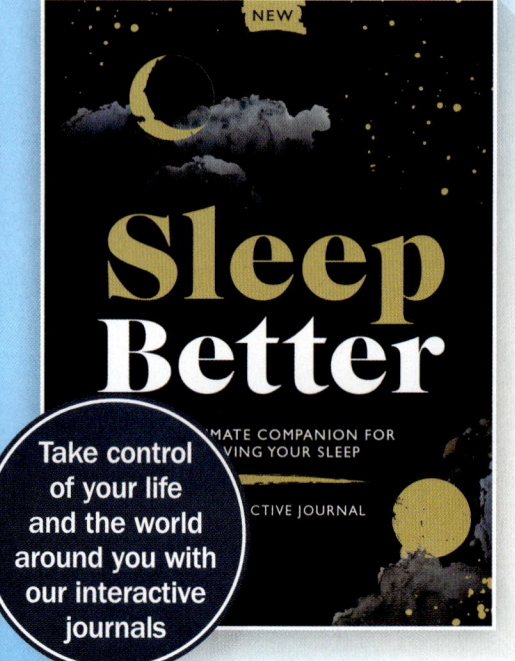

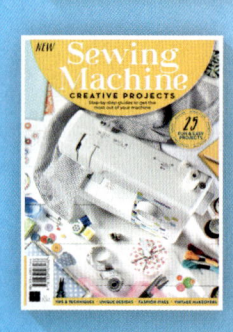

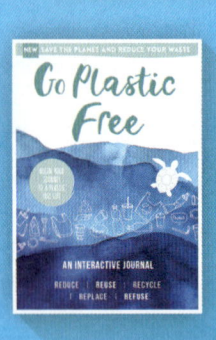

Discover adventures of a lifetime with our inspiring travel books

Take control of your life and the world around you with our interactive journals

Get essential advice on how to make positive changes to your health and wellbeing

✓ Get great savings when you buy direct from us

✓ 1000s of great titles, many not available anywhere else

✓ World-wide delivery and super-safe ordering

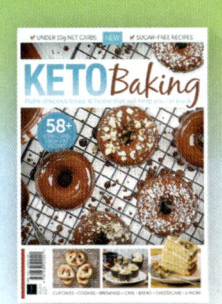

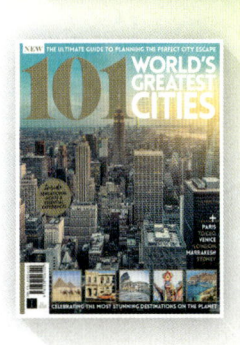

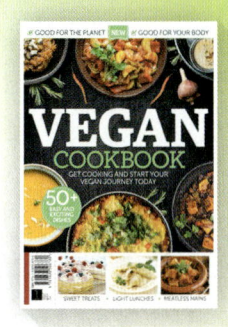

INSPIRING READS FOR A HAPPIER YOU

From travel and food to mindfulness and fitness, discover motivational books to enrich and enhance your life

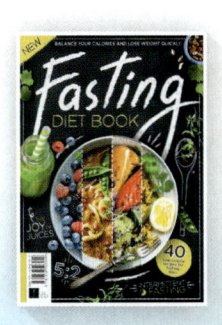

Learn delicious recipes and nutritional information for all tastes and lifestyles

Follow us on Instagram @futurebookazines

www.magazinesdirect.com
Magazines, back issues & bookazines.

SUBSCRIBE & SAVE UP TO 61%

Delivered direct to your door or straight to your device

Choose from over 80 magazines and make great savings off the store price!

Binders, books and back issues also available

Simply visit www.magazinesdirect.com

✓ No hidden costs   🚚 Shipping included in all prices   🌐 We deliver to over 100 countries   🔒 Secure online payment

FUTURE

magazinesdirect.com
Official Magazine Subscription Store